Modern American Housing

New City Books

The New City Books series explores the intersection of architecture, landscape architecture, infrastructure, and planning in the redevelopment of the civic realm. Focusing on government sponsorship of design, the study of weak-market cities, contemporary American housing, and the role of a research university as a resource and collaborator, the series highlights the formative nature of innovative design and the necessity for strategies that trigger public and private support.

The New City Books series includes:

From the Ground Up
Innovative Green Homes

Formerly Urban
Projecting Rust Belt Futures

New Public Works
Architecture, Planning, and Politics

Modern American Housing
High-Rise, Reuse, Infill

American City "X"
Syracuse after the Master Plan

Modern American Housing

High-Rise, Reuse, Infill

Edited by Peggy Tully

With contributions by
Andrew Bernheimer
Julie Eizenberg
Jonathan Massey
Gregg Pasquarelli, Vishaan
Chakrabarti, Douglas Gauthier,
and Philip Nobel
Mark Robbins
Stanley Saitowitz

Syracuse University
School of Architecture
and
Princeton Architectural Press

Published by
Princeton Architectural Press
37 East Seventh Street
New York, New York 10003
Visit our website at www.papress.com.

Syracuse University School of Architecture
Slocum Hall
Syracuse, New York 13244
www.soa.syr.edu

Series Editor: Mark Robbins

Design: Pentagram

Project Editor: Dan Simon

Special thanks to: Sara Bader, Meredith Baber,
Janet Behning, Nicola Bednarek Brower,
Fannie Bushin, Megan Carey, Carina Cha,
Andrea Chlad, Benjamin English, Russell
Fernandez, Jan Haux, Diane Levinson, Jennifer
Lippert, Katharine Myers, Margaret Rogalski,
Elana Schlenker, Sara Stemen, Andrew
Stepanian, Paul Wagner, and Joseph Weston
of Princeton Architectural Press
—Kevin C. Lippert, publisher

The New City Books series is made possible
by a grant from the Rockefeller Foundation.
Additional funding is provided by the
Syracuse University School of Architecture,
Judith Greenberg Seinfeld, the National
Endowment for the Arts, The Richard H.
Driehaus Foundation, the Graham Foundation
for Advanced Studies in the Fine Arts, the
New York State Council for the Arts, Deutsche
Bank Americas Foundation, Furthermore:
a program of the J. M. Kaplan Fund, and the
Central New York Community Foundation.

Library of Congress
Cataloging-in-Publication Data

Modern American housing: high-rise,
reuse, infill / edited by Peggy Tully; with
contributions by Andrew Bernheimer [and
seven others]. — First edition.

pages cm — (New city books)

Includes bibliographical references.

ISBN 978-1-61689-109-1 (hardcover: alk. paper)

1. Architecture, Domestic—United States—
History—21st century—Case studies. 2.
Architecture and society—United States—
History—21st century. I. Tully, Peggy, editor of
compilation.

NA7208.2.M63 2013

728.0973'09051—dc23

2012024510

Contents

Preface and Acknowledgments

The home defines us, and the way we are housed is central to our self-image and culture. While always addressing market imperatives in terms of land use and form, housing is at one end of the spectrum obsessed with style and formal pattern-making, at the other with regulation and normative concepts of family. This book explores a range of contemporary American housing grouped according to three common typologies found in both small and large cities: high-rise, reuse, and infill.

The concept for the publication evolved from three visiting critic studios at the Syracuse University School of Architecture. The studios focused on these three building types, employing a case-study format as the basis for each studio's design courses. Jared Della Valle and Andy Bernheimer of Della Valle Bernheimer based their studio on a high-rise site in the Hudson Yards of New York City that was an actual site for their firm; Julie Eizenberg of Koning Eizenberg Architecture set her project within the context of the renovation of an abandoned warehouse in downtown Syracuse; and Stanley Saitowitz of Stanley Saitowitz/Natoma Architects activated a variety of infill sites located along the expansion of the BART system in San Francisco. These studios sought to explore and bring together the most enlightened thinking about various forms of housing and other commercial types of development that might be engaged as they define our culture and revitalize our urban centers. Each architect approached the pedagogy of the studio in a different way and contributed an essay to this publication; they also, like curators of urban design, suggested projects that exemplify national models.

The suite of three studios and this publication were made possible through the generous support of Judith Greenberg Seinfeld, a Syracuse University trustee and an advisory board member of the School of Architecture. She understood the importance of giving students the tools to participate broadly in making and remaking our cities. We are appreciative of her vision and commitment to the work of the School and the University.

The New City Books series, of which this publication is a part, is made possible by a grant from the Rockefeller Foundation. Additional funding is provided by the Syracuse University School of Architecture, the National Endowment for the Arts, The Richard H. Driehaus Foundation, the Graham Foundation for Advanced Studies in the Fine Arts, the New York State Council for the Arts, Deutsche Bank Americas Foundation, Furthermore: a program of the J. M. Kaplan Fund, and the Central New York Community Foundation. We are grateful to all of these funders for their support.

This book would not have been possible without a committed group at the School of Architecture. Many thanks to Peggy Tully, a research fellow at UPSTATE: A Center for Design, Research, and Real Estate and the book's editor, and to Nilus Klingel, Syracuse University Engagement Fellow, for all his hard work and positive attitude. For their encouragement and support of the New City Books series, I would like to thank Julia Czerniak, Assistant Dean Katryn Hansen, and Mary Kate O'Brien, director of communications and media relations.

Thanks also go to Jennifer Lippert and Kevin Lippert at Princeton Architectural Press for their interest in the New City Books series and its ambitions, and to Megan Carey and Dan Simon at PAPress. The design of the books was especially important given the topic, and the way they look and read is the outcome of many productive conversations with Michael Bierut and Pentagram. I am grateful for Michael's calm intellect and wit throughout the process, as well as for the graphic talents of designer Hamish Smyth. Finally, I am thankful to Karen Stein for her intellect and counsel in developing the series as a whole, and to Kate Norment, who kept us all on track with a steady yet firm hand. This entire team has become a small community, without which this book and this series could not have come into being.

We hope that this publication raises a greater awareness of the interdependence of architecture and the marketplace and adds to the dialogue between architects and those in the development, finance, and real estate fields in addressing the issue of housing, the obstacles to its production, and the mechanisms by which innovative strategies can be employed across these communities.

Mark Robbins
Former dean, Syracuse University School of Architecture

Risk and Regulation in the Financial Architecture of American Houses

Jonathan Massey

What is a house? Among other things, it is an instrument for distributing economic risk and opportunity among individuals and institutions.

Although it is often seen as a stable foundation for home life and household finance, the house is equally an unstable commodity affording its owners the opportunity for profit and the risk of loss. In the United States, two of three owner-occupied houses serve as collateral for the mortgage loan that made the house purchase possible. Through mortgage financing, American houses mediate our relation to state and market, integrating us into global credit markets beyond the scope of everyday awareness and instilling disciplines that shape our conduct. Our houses mediate between the microeconomics of household finance and the macroeconomic forces of a globalized economy.

House design and construction are governed by zoning codes and building codes, of course, but they are also regulated by tax codes and institutional practices that encourage some kinds of consumption and discourage others by assessing them at different rates. Expenditures on housing are subject to this kind of sumptuary regulation through tax provisions, such as the mortgage interest deduction, and institutional supports, such as the mortgage insurance provided by the Federal Housing Administration (FHA). The lending, underwriting, and insurance assessment practices of the FHA, other bureaucracies, and banks affect the balances between risk and opportunity in homeownership and between convention and innovation in house design.[1]

The regulatory regime governing the consumption of houses has evolved significantly over the past century, and this modernization of housing finance has influenced both the design and the social meaning of houses. This history has four major periods linked to cycles of boom and bust in the real estate market and the larger economy.

As the twentieth century began, the laissez-faire state provided little support for homeownership apart from the homesteading provisions in land policy, and credit markets were small and localized. After World

War I, collaboration between the state and real estate interests during the economic surge of the 1920s forged an "associational state" that expanded access to credit and began to integrate the mortgage finance market at a national scale. The interventionist state that emerged from the Depression and the New Deal established a highly regulated, state-supported national mortgage market that shaped American houses, neighborhoods, and land-use patterns up to the oil shock of the early 1970s. From the mid-1970s until the mortgage-triggered global financial crisis that began in 2007, market innovations and the globalization of finance combined to outpace and undermine the existing regulatory regime as Keynesianism yielded to neoliberalism as a prevalent political ideology.[2] During each of these periods, new lending institutions and practices reshaped the role of the house in mediating among individual, state, and market to manage the changing needs of an evolving capitalist economy.

The Laissez-Faire State

A mortgage is a loan secured by real property in which the buyer transfers all or part of his or her interest in the property to the lender as collateral on the condition that this interest be returned to the owner when the terms

of the loan have been met. Mortgage lending practices and laws have established a system that negotiates the risks and opportunities of both lenders and borrowers. Though the mortgage has served since antiquity as a legal instrument for financing homeownership, its terms and financial structure have varied across both time and space.[3]

The mortgage loan was fundamental to the expansion of the American middle class in the twentieth century, and as historians Michael Doucet and John Weaver have observed, its significance in shaping North American cities and their buildings is comparable to that of the subdivided lot and the balloon frame. In the late nineteenth century, the residential development process in the United States was decentralized, barely regulated, and poorly coordinated. For most purchasers, buying a house required complex and uncertain credit arrangements. Housing was largely custom built, and families often built their own homes. Some who could not turned for assistance to small-scale operative builders, who rarely completed more than a few houses per year. Homeownership was often precarious and was typically achieved incrementally by tapping local networks organized through personal and ethnic affiliations.

Daniel Kariko, *Club House, I-4 Corridor* (opposite) and *Lost Roads, Central Florida* (above), 2009, aerial photographs of a partly completed subdivision near Lakeland, Florida, from the series SpeculationWorld

Capital for individuals and families wishing to purchase or build houses was very limited, and it usually came from individuals, as banks limited their risk exposure by focusing on short-term loans to commercial concerns, such as traders and wholesalers. Potential buyers had to accumulate large sums in order to make the high down payments needed to purchase a house. Most people lived in rented housing; the homeownership rate was 46 percent in 1900.[4] For many owner-borrowers, the employment stability and savings pattern necessary to pay off a mortgage were elusive.

The development of a house usually began with its future occupant's purchase of a building lot, either from savings or through short-term financing, such as a one- to five-year mortgage from a family member, friend, or, less often, a life insurance company or bank. Most loans were balloon loans, in which the borrower made interest-only payments annually or semiannually, with the full principal of the loan—the balloon—due at the end of the term. The borrower could then repeat the process at a larger scale, offering the property as collateral on another balloon mortgage for the funds with which to build a house. Individual mortgage loans typically constituted no more than 30 to 40 percent of the assessed property value, with loan terms rarely exceeding five or six years. Buyers with limited capital frequently resorted to higher-interest second and third mortgages, or junior mortgages, to bridge whatever funding gap remained once their primary loan and down payment were factored in.[5]

Ideally, the borrower accumulated enough savings during the term of a balloon loan to pay off the mortgage when it came due. In practice, however, this was difficult, and loan renewals were the norm. While this system worked well during boom times, when confidence was high and holders of capital were eager to lend, it tended to intensify downturns and financial panics, as lenders would call in a loan at the end of its term. The scarcity of capital and the complexity of assembling large-scale financing in this era meant that real estate developers found it difficult to develop large subdivisions complete with houses, so speculators usually divided land into lots, cut streets, and then began to sell off house lots in small batches to families and operative builders.

There was no national mortgage market in this era. Instead, credit was furnished through hundreds of local markets, with varying lending policies, interest rates, and regulation by different state laws. Since the 1830s, entrepreneurs and civic leaders had begun forming mutual savings banks that pooled member savings for mortgage investment. But with demand for capital higher than these fledgling institutions could supply, the larger

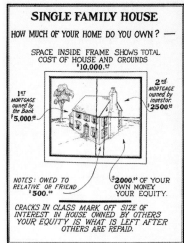

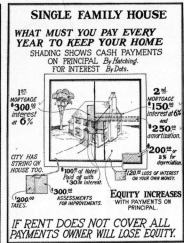

cities evolved mortgage markets made up of thousands of small investors, lending in small quantities for short terms. Mortgage brokers and real
estate agents linked these small investors and borrowers through webs of
personal acquaintance and informal market knowledge. Accordingly, credit
was differentially available to consumers based in part on their race, ethnic
origin, and gender. Polish American residents of Milwaukee, for instance,
like members of other immigrant ethnic communities in the industrial
cities, supplemented their savings with loans from local, ethnically based
lending circles. In Polish neighborhoods, these were known as *skarbi*, or
"treasuries." Members of such communities frequently built houses room
by room, through additions and expansions as families struggled to finance
construction within stringent lending terms.[6]

Despite its broad diffusion of agency, this development system yielded
a high degree of architectural consistency within regional and local
housing markets through what historian Sam Bass Warner called market-
driven "regulation without laws." The late nineteenth-century suburban
neighborhoods of Boston that formed the basis of Warner's research were
made up of lots and blocks developed and built out by different owners
and investors, creating mixed and variable urban fabrics. These patches
were integrated by gridded street planning, however—and also by adherence to traditional and popular patterns in the planning and design of
houses, chosen by the many homeowners and small investors betting
all or most of their capital on construction of a house. Disciplined by risk
to make conservative choices, these house builders imitated one another
in their decisions about type, size, siting, and style. At the same time,

Arthur C. Holden, *Primer of Housing*,
1927, illustrations explaining
multiple-mortgage financing and
homeownership costs

the small scale of decision making and construction yielded extensive variety in the specific elaboration and detailing of those familiar forms.[7]

The Associational State

World War I prompted the first direct interventions in the housing market by the federal government. Wartime command provisions severely limited housing construction, and a postwar recession exacerbated the freeze. Identifying a shortage of housing as the problem, real estate interests organized to stimulate the production and consumption of houses.

In 1918 the National Association of Real Estate Brokers joined with the U.S. Department of Labor and lumber companies to sponsor a nationwide campaign of advertising, publications, and exhibitions urging consumers to buy houses. This and other homeownership campaigns promoted the idea that the house was a special kind of commodity, one worth the risk attendant on investing a substantial down payment and going into debt. They were part of a process that real estate historian Jeffrey Hornstein has called "dreaming the American home," through which the house became "a sustained focus of scientific, technical, reformist, political, and business discourse," in the process coming to symbolize ideals of family life and citizenship.[8]

As commerce secretary in the 1920s, then as president during the early 1930s, Herbert Hoover promoted a moral economy of the home that centered on the house as both an artifact and a site of consumption. Shortly after becoming secretary of commerce in 1921, Hoover founded the Division of Building and Housing to promote standardization and efficiency by collaborating with industry groups to standardize and simplify building codes, real estate contracts, and zoning. After Marie Mattingly (Mrs. W. B.) Meloney, the editor of *Delineator* magazine, launched a national campaign to promote better houses, Hoover embraced her movement as a counterpart to his own initiatives, and he helped formalize Meloney's Better Homes in America (BHA) as an educational foundation with professional leadership and headquarters in Washington, D.C.[9]

Modernizing housing finance was a key focus of these housing initiatives. Under Hoover, the U.S. Department of Commerce promoted homeownership through pamphlets and other publications, while BHA set out "to encourage thrift for home ownership, and to spread knowledge of methods of financing the purchase or building of a home." The organization sponsored lectures and pamphlets on various topics, with titles such as "How to Own Your Home" and "Financing the Small Home."[10]

Changes in the sources and terms of loan funds supplemented the older forms of familial lending and ethnic association and spurred an expansion of mortgage lending in the 1920s. Building and loan associations—since the 1930s called savings and loan associations—had emerged in the 1880s, and by the 1920s they had become a significant source of capital for home builders and home buyers. These institutions pooled the savings of individuals, then lent these savings funds to member-investors who were buying or building a house. They epitomized Hoover's vision of the associational state, in which economic sectors would be rationalized and regulated through voluntary cooperation among trade associations rather than by the state.

Building and loan associations introduced more generous lending practices, such as eleven- and twelve-year loan terms, as well as amortization, under which the borrower made monthly payments that blended interest charges with partial principal payments and sometimes even tax and insurance payments. In this way, principal was paid off incrementally, reducing the risk of default by inculcating in homeowners a strict month-to-month fiscal discipline. Blended-payment amortization constituted a fiscal discipline that helped make homeownership a savings practice. Though they typically charged slightly higher interest rates than did conventional banks, building and loan associations also lent a higher proportion of the cost—60 to 75 percent of the assessed home value, as opposed to the 50 percent common among lending banks. This increase in the loan-to-value ratio meant that a home loan required a smaller down payment and the homeowner was less likely to need additional mortgage loans at higher rates. Building and loan associations were also more willing than other lenders to extend capital for the risky process of house construction.[11]

The lending terms of building and loan associations made mortgages more accessible to borrowers and more stable for investors. A U.S. Census Bureau study conducted in 1923 showed that while the homeownership rate had remained steady over the preceding decades, the terms of ownership had changed markedly: between 1890 and 1920, the percentage of mortgaged homes had increased by more than one-third, from 28 to 38 percent, and the ratio of debt to home value had risen as borrowers increasingly tapped institutional rather than individual lending sources. "Today the building and loan association is the working man's way par excellence of achieving a home," wrote Robert S. Lynd and Helen Merrell Lynd, authors of the sociological study *Middletown* (1929). In Muncie, Indiana, which the Lynds studied as a typical middle-American city, four building and loan associations together financed an estimated 75 to 80 percent of new houses in the peak year of 1925.[12]

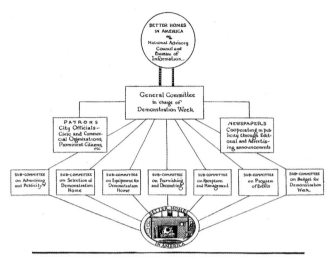

Better Homes in America
organizational chart for
demonstration week, 1922

Ray H. Bennett Lumber Co.,
Inc., *Bennett Homes: Better-
Built Ready-Cut*, catalog 18,
1920, page featuring the Dover,
a compact three-bedroom,
one-bath bungalow sold as a kit
of prefabricated parts for on-site
construction by a local builder

Dover

26 ft. x 36 ft. over all
6 Rooms and Bath

The Dover is a splendid example of how the all-on-one-floor bungalow home can luxuriously and comfortably house a large family.

In appearance, this home is ideally balanced. Graceful roof lines blend into its shingled sides. Porch pillars carry through the idea of substantiality. Overhanging eaves give the final touch to the bungalow theme.

Let us analyze the Dover from the viewpoint of solid comfort. The twenty-six foot porch promises plenty of outdoor comfort and air. The living room provides space for not only the whole family but several guests in addition. The dining room is large enough to accommodate a holiday dinner party. In case of large entertainments, the two rooms can practically be opened into one. The three bedrooms suffice for a family of five or six—or with less people, a guest room is available.

There's a kitchen ample for all needs.

You may have noticed where you can build a fireplace in the living room. That bay in the dining room you can plan for flowers and plants, or just a cozy cushioned seat. You have made a note of that celebrated step-saver, the kitchen cabinet. Did you see the closets for each sleeping room?

If it's a bungalow home that meets your fondest wishes, and the Dover satisfies your needs, then we can assure you that it will be ideal.

SPECIFICATIONS

Ceiling height first floor approximately 9 ft.
Girders 6 in. x 6 in.
First floor joists 2 in. x 8 in.
Ceiling joists 2 in. x 4 in. Rafters 2 in. x 6 in.
Ceiling joists plan B 2 in. x 6 in.
Front door—special design, 3 ft. x 6 ft. 8 in. and
1¾ in. thick, glazed.
French doors between living room and dining room.
Our kitchen cupboard No. 2 and medicine cabinet
included in the selling price. *See pages 36–37.*
Attic stairs and flooring included in the selling price
of plan B.

See pages 8–9 for general specifications.

50

These new financing mechanisms combined with changes in design and construction to engender a new way of consuming the house, which became by the mid-1920s a consumer durable accessible to a wider range of buyers through normalized, liberalized credit. The 1910s and 1920s saw the rise of the smaller yet more intensively serviced house, reformatted to control price in an age of rising costs in construction and land, as well as to reflect declining family size. Though houses were smaller, with fewer rooms overall and fewer special-purpose rooms, such as a library or a parlor, they were more likely to be equipped with modern services and equipment: central heating, automatic heating with thermostatic control, electricity, automatic refrigeration, running water, modern plumbing. As the nation's economy shifted from an agricultural base to an industrial and corporate one, home production of food, clothing, and other goods yielded to consumption of factory-made and store-bought items, and something similar happened with houses. Rather than being built and equipped incrementally by enterprising owners, they were more often built all at once or purchased as a finished artifact—a commodity.

These changes were thematized in the demonstration houses built and exhibited by local Better Homes chapters from 1923 into the mid-1930s during the annual ritual of national Better Homes Week, when local chapters orchestrated programs promoting homeownership. The focus of these events was usually the showcasing of houses built or renovated to serve as examples of good house design and home culture. During the first national campaign, in 1923, local chapters in fifty-seven cities and towns built or remodeled a total of seventy-eight demonstration houses. In the 1929 campaign, of the nearly 6,000 committees participating, 269 reported showing a total of 532 houses.[13]

An especially well-documented case is that of Everyman's House, a compact yet carefully worked-out demonstration house built in 1924 by the Kalamazoo, Michigan, chapter. Designed by Caroline Bartlett Crane, a doctor's wife who had organized local and statewide home-ownership initiatives, and detailed for construction by architect Gilbert Worden, Everyman's House adapted a traditional American house form—the colonial revival cottage—to the changing needs of middle- and working-class families, as well as to the availability of longer-term amortized loans from building and loan associations. Its purpose was to promote homeownership by showing "the best possibilities in home-building and home-equipment at a cost within the reach of a large number of non-home-owning people," estimated at around $5,000.[14] By publishing a book on the subject of the house, Crane spread its

Caroline Bartlett Crane with
Gilbert Worden, Everyman's
House, Kalamazoo, Michigan, 1924.
Promotional photograph of the
Everymans at dinner

fame well beyond Kalamazoo and laid out the ideological dimensions
of Better Homes Week.

Everyman's House incorporated many features of the smaller,
better-serviced house, such as a living room with a dining alcove and
an efficiently planned kitchen with built-in fixtures and appliances.
But an equally significant dimension of its modernity was its highlighting
of the new possibilities in home finance. Crane pointed out that the high
cost and geographical fixity of housing had the value of stabilizing workers
and bringing them into the middle-class social and political imaginary.
She saw homeownership as a way to reduce political dissatisfaction with
America's capitalist economy by increasing the proportion of Americans
who owned property and so had a stake in maintaining the existing social
order. By helping them "achieve a home," Crane explained, Everyman's
House promised to give them "a vital stake in government." Along with
the "sense of dignity in belonging to the social order" that came with
homeownership, Everyman would acquire "respect for organized industry
and for the law-regulated institutions of finance which furnish him the

employment and insurance and credit necessary for the building of that home. Home-owning and Bolshevism," she concluded, "are just naturally strangers." Crane echoed the rhetoric of Hoover and the many other proponents of homeownership who saw it as the basis of good citizenship or even, as the slogan of the U.S. League of Local Building and Home Associations put it, "the safeguard of American liberties" in the face of crises such as World War I, the postwar recession, and the Red Scare.[15]

The wage laborer aspiring to homeownership, Crane asserted, "must not be casual or peripatetic. He must be both willing and able to anchor in a home of some sort and become a part of the community."[16] By joining a building and loan association, she explained, a lot owner could expect to use the property as collateral in obtaining a loan for up to 80 percent of the construction cost of Everyman's House, with a twelve-year term at just under 7 percent interest. In some especially progressive cities, private lending associations specializing in short-term second mortgages could help provide financing to bridge any remaining gap between the borrower's savings and the costs in excess of the first mortgage amount.

Caroline Bartlett Crane with Gilbert Worden, Everyman's House, Kalamazoo, Michigan, 1924, street view with Everyman's House at right

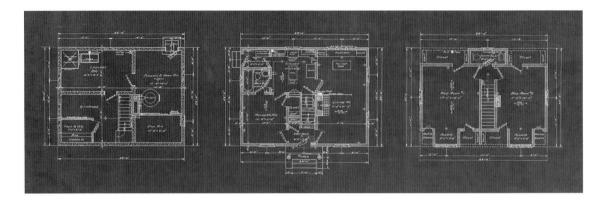

Caroline Bartlett Crane with Gilbert Worden, Everyman's House, Kalamazoo, Michigan, 1924, plans

Everyman's House—like most new houses in an era of increasing mortgage indebtedness—was an anchor tying working families to place and polity through credit obligations. By cultivating a new set of bonds, dependencies, and disciplines in its purchaser, Everyman's House promoted a yeoman ideal of American citizenship even as it reflected the transformation of the house from a place of production to one of consumption within an industrial capitalist order.

Studies of the building industry during the 1920s showed that only at the very high end did architects design a large proportion of projects. One architecture journal estimated the rate of "architectural control" as dropping from 95 percent among the top two-thirds of 1 percent of houses by cost, through 78 percent of the next 2 percent of houses, to a mere 15 percent of the remaining 97 percent—those costing less than $20,000. Concerned about this low market share, architects sought to gain traction in the market for small, lower-cost houses, particularly those in the $5,000 to $10,000 range. Many entered competitions dedicated to recognizing good examples of affordable houses, including annual BHA competitions. The Architects' Small House Service Bureau, a nonprofit corporation founded in Minneapolis in 1920, promoted the use of architect-generated designs in the small-house market. Endorsed by both the American Institute of Architects and the Department of Commerce under Hoover, the bureau sold stock plans that owners, contractors, and architects could use in low-cost projects where an architect's design services posed a prohibitive cost, publishing the stock plans in its magazine, *The Small Home*.[17]

Some architects challenged the prevailing emphasis on building new single-family houses as the solution. Frederick L. Ackerman, an architect and policy analyst who emerged in the 1920s as a leading voice for

socialization of the housing field, contended that the major problem in housing was not a shortage of units but shortcomings in financial accessibility to families of low and moderate incomes. Ackerman argued that the practices of market-based development, speculative investment, and difficult financing systematically withheld housing from potential occupants in order to maintain high profit margins. Before World War I had even ended, Ackerman and other progressives began promoting government-built, multiunit social housing as a superior postwar alternative to market-based development and the single-family house. Their solutions included not only new principles in planning and design but also alternative mechanisms of ownership and financing to circumvent the complex and costly system of a high down payment and multiple mortgages, such as state development and ownership of housing, state financing of cooperative associations, the formation of nonprofit community land companies funded through bond issuance, and tax exemptions for housing developments that reflected progressive garden city ideals.[18]

Contractor Herbert Richheimer referring to a model of a Levittown housing development during a sales meeting, 1957

The Interventionist State

The Great Depression spurred more direct federal intervention in the homeownership market. As the economy shrank after the stock market collapse in 1929, lenders began to demand repayment of short-term balloon loans when they came due, rather than grant the renewals that had been customary in better times, and this triggered foreclosures. Property values fell, in many cases below the value of the debt the properties had secured, and some properties became unmarketable. In Muncie, where some 63 percent of owner-occupied homes were mortgaged, foreclosures rose from an estimated ten or fewer in 1928 to more than one hundred in 1934. "It was our fault for overselling them," said one of the city's real estate agents, "and the banks' fault for overlending. Everybody was buying a better home than he could afford."

The expansion of homeownership through the liberalization of credit had afforded a large proportion of the population the opportunity of investment in homeownership but also exposed it to the risks of borrowing against such an expensive, fluctuating asset as a house.[19]

As banks withdrew from mortgage lending, Congress and President Hoover established new programs and agencies dedicated to improving the residential loan market. These included the Home Owners' Loan Corporation and the Federal Home Loan Bank Board, a federally coordinated network of mortgage lenders following uniform lending standards and drawing on a common credit pool. Franklin D. Roosevelt's New Deal greatly expanded the federal role, implementing through government authority the policies that Hoover's administration had proposed for voluntary industry adoption. The National Housing Act of June 1934 established the Federal Housing Administration (FHA) to provide mutual mortgage insurance on houses and low-cost housing projects. It also authorized the FHA to charter national mortgage associations—the first of which would be the Federal National Mortgage Association (Fannie Mae) in 1938—to buy and sell FHA-insured mortgages, thereby establishing a secondary market to furnish greater liquidity for mortgage capital.[20]

The FHA diminished the risk of mortgage finance for both lenders and borrowers, and it fostered closer adherence to convention in residential development and design. In order to qualify for FHA insurance, a mortgage loan and the property that secured it—as well as both borrower and lender—had to meet criteria laid out by the agency. Mortgages insured by the FHA typically featured higher loan-to-value ratios than had loans in the 1920s, with longer terms (fifteen years at first, though terms rapidly lengthened until thirty years became the norm) and blended-payment amortization.

The incentive of inexpensive federal insurance led lenders, borrowers, and builders to adopt FHA standards quickly. The insurance protection, along with the homogenization it fostered, in turn allowed investors anywhere in the country to purchase a mortgage loan with greater confidence in its basic soundness, and Fannie Mae spurred the market by purchasing insured mortgages from the primary lenders. These interventions rapidly created a national market in mortgage finance. In this way, housing entered the emerging mixed economy shaped by both government regulation and market action. Instead of socializing housing production, as Ackerman and others had advocated, the National Housing Act socialized risk.[21]

The impact of the National Housing Act was rapid and profound. Housing starts rose 40 percent in 1934, 70 percent in 1935, and 50 percent in 1936; and during the second half of the 1930s, one in four nonfarm dwellings added to national inventory was financed by an FHA mortgage. By 1940 the monthly payment plan that went along with FHA insurance had become "the accepted mode of financing home repairs and home purchases in most communities," and FHA-insured houses had become typical of new construction in the nation's 140 largest housing markets. State insurance of mortgage loans through the FHA, loan guarantees from the Veterans Administration (VA) after World War II, and guarantee of the secondary market in mortgage debt through Fannie Mae allowed builders, brokers, and consumers to speculate more reliably in housing development.[22]

FHA underwriting policies—the criteria whereby the agency assessed the soundness of a mortgage and the value and creditworthiness of the house that served as its collateral—soon became prescriptive for developers, purchasers, and lenders alike, and they favored large tract developments consisting primarily of single-family houses on lower-cost land on the edges of developed metropolitan areas. The new regulatory regime of federal loan insurance and guarantees was geared to institutional lenders and a new tier of large merchant builders or community builders, companies that handled the entire development process from land acquisition and subdivision through construction to marketing.[23]

These new subdivisions were epitomized by the large-scale developments built in New York, New Jersey, and Pennsylvania by the Levitt brothers. Geared to FHA and VA financing, these Levittowns consisted of raised ranch and Cape Cod cottage designs, and came with refrigerators, stoves, and even televisions, which were included in the purchase price and amortized into the mortgage. Modernist designs, as the FHA cautioned in a technical bulletin advising underwriters, sometimes carried extra risk in resale and valuation because of potential "nonconformity" between the aesthetics of the house and its residential purpose, or between the house and neighboring properties in terms of siting and aesthetics. Large-scale financing, development, construction, and marketing of houses produced homogeneous neighborhoods of nearly identical houses designed largely to meet FHA criteria and retain their resale value throughout the thirty-year loan term.[24] In this way, the sumptuary regime initiated by the New Deal promoted construction of single-family house types, such as the saltbox, the colonial cottage, and the ranch house, integrated into large-scale developments.

The parameters that the FHA, Fannie Mae, and other institutions established for the planning, design, construction, and financing of houses stabilized the role of housing as a means of capital accumulation for institutional investors and house purchasers alike, boosting the postwar homeownership rate to nearly 70 percent. At the same time, FHA underwriting guidelines, market assumptions, and federal policy led many lenders to redline neighborhoods with significant minority populations so that racial segregation was built into the formation of the middle class and its built environment through selective extension of credit and the risk-based pricing of mortgage loans.[25]

The Globalized Credit Market

From the early 1970s to 2007, the globalization of credit markets and a worldwide economic boom coincided with innovations that expanded the range, flexibility, and scale of mortgage financing. This combination diminished state regulation, increased both opportunity and risk, introduced new house designs, and shifted the culture of homeownership toward a model that was more entrepreneurial than the one that had prevailed during the postwar period.

After the oil shock of 1973, inflation raised house prices, making homeownership more challenging but also a potentially more rewarding investment. Many consumers began investing a greater proportion of their money in housing, buying larger and more expensive houses as a way to turn their homes into speculative investments. The nation's mortgage-lending capacity, meanwhile, was augmented by the growth of the secondary market in mortgage debt through federal intervention, loan securitization, and a proliferation of new loan types.

In the late 1960s the federal government restructured Fannie Mae and created the Government National Mortgage Association (Ginnie Mae) and the Federal Home Loan Mortgage Corporation (Freddie Mac) to expand the supply of mortgage credit by purchasing government-issued and market-issued mortgages; by 2008 the government owned or guaranteed nearly half of the nation's total outstanding home mortgage debt. Computerization allowed banks and other investors to securitize mortgages by batching many loans into large debt pools generating monthly income streams, then selling securities backed by narrow slices of the aggregated debt. With the nation's housing stock extensively conforming to FHA underwriting standards and federal or quasi-federal insurance protecting most loans, mortgage-backed securities seemed like nearly risk-free investments. Institutional investors around the world, including

central banks, pension funds, and commercial banks, saw the federally regulated American mortgage market as a low-risk, high-yield investment opportunity, especially when credit-rating agencies began rating mortgage-backed securities. In this way, securitization in the secondary mortgage market created new linkages between individual consumers and global capital markets.[26]

Capital flooded the residential mortgage market as American home finance became globalized. Lenders expanded their market by offering a range of new loan types, including jumbo loans, which were larger than the maximum amount insured by the FHA; forty-year loan terms; the reborn junior mortgage in the form of piggyback loans; and adjustable-rate

The teardown cycle as played out in Annandale, Virginia, in 2004: a postwar two-bedroom, one-bath slab-on-grade asbestos-shingled house prior to teardown (top), and a McMansion under construction on the same lot (bottom)

Daniel Kariko, #103 Lehigh Acres, 2009, photograph of an unmaintained tract house near Lakeland, Florida, from the series SpeculationWorld

mortgages. Rising house values allowed many homeowners to finance renovations, additions, or other expenditures unrelated to housing by borrowing against the inflated house value through home equity loans, which afforded lenders and borrowers alike another way to increase volume, profit opportunities, and risk.

The combination of rising house prices and the influx of global credit encouraged some finance companies in the 1990s to extend credit for transactions that did not qualify for federal insurance. Because taking on such subprime cases entailed assuming greater risk, these firms usually charged higher interest rates and higher loan-origination fees. While such risk-based pricing expanded access to credit for borrowers, including for minority borrowers traditionally excluded from the market by redlining, it soon took a high toll as lenders introduced a raft of high-risk loan types that dispensed with key elements in FHA underwriting assessments. Since many loan originators and brokers realized a quick profit by reselling their loans for securitization in the secondary market, loan amounts frequently exceeded even optimistic property valuations, as investment pressure in the credit market outpaced price inflation of the houses serving as collateral. Through these mechanisms, borrowers and creditors alike entered into an imprudent partnership of real estate speculation that yielded large profits but carried sizable risks.[27]

The rise in house prices had been accompanied by little change in income levels, and the median house price, long two to three times the median annual income, had risen to some four times the median income. When house prices began to fall in many markets in 2005 and 2006, subprime borrowers began to default at an accelerating rate. As had happened in the late 1920s and early 1930s, defaults triggered a sudden contraction in the credit market.

Securitization had obscured the extent of subprime lending and had blended subprime loans into the larger pool of standard mortgages so that nearly all investors in the credit markets had some risk exposure. In replacing traditionally bilateral mortgage lending with multilateral transactions, securitization also intensified the likelihood of foreclosure by making it difficult for debtors and creditors to modify loan terms and craft the consensual workarounds that in the Depression had miti- gated the negative consequences of default for borrower and lender alike. The interconnectedness created by securitization, meanwhile, spread the consequences of the real estate downturn into other economic sectors, triggering a worldwide economic recession. Once again, the federal government assumed a large volume in losses, socializing costs after years of private profit taking, this time in order to protect investment banks as well as Fannie Mae and Freddie Mac. Many of the economic and social costs of the bust were thus absorbed not by the market participants but by the broader taxpayer base.

Prior to the credit crisis, however, homeownership became an attrac- tive way for middle-class consumers to speculate on credit. Even as the average household size dwindled, the average size of a new single-family house increased from 1,660 square feet in 1973 to 2,521 in 2007. The value of new houses rose dramatically as well, from an average of $62,500 in 1978 to $313,600 in 2007.[28] The expanded range of loan products supported innovation by financing improvements to old inner-city houses that failed to meet FHA underwriting requirements; construction and resale of houses with inflated values that exceeded FHA insurance limits; and construction of new houses, town houses, and condominium units tailored to niche markets, such as post–baby boom empty nesters.

Among the architectural dimensions of these changes was the rise of large tract houses sometimes derided as McMansions. These houses of 3,000 to 5,000 square feet typically occupy a high proportion of their suburban or exurban lot, their bulk articulated by complex rooflines. Though laden with signifiers of wealth, such as high-ceilinged foyers and great rooms, they lack the construction quality and design detailing of the older or more expensive houses they evoke. Another result of the changed finance market was the teardown, in which a homeowner used savings and home equity credit to demolish an existing house and build a larger one with more luxurious finishes and updated services, typically on a valuable inner-suburb lot. Prompted as they were by financial rather than physical obsolescence, such teardowns highlighted the centrality of financing to the architecture of American houses.

The mortgage-supported real estate speculation of the 1990s and the early years of the twenty-first century was captured in a spate of television shows built around the culture of house flipping: the practice of purchasing and improving a house, then reselling it at a higher price. As long as prices continued to rise, astute homeowners could use credit to finance a series of transactions that netted them a good profit even once the transaction and renovation costs were deducted from the sale price. Television series titles included *Flip This House, Flip That House, Property Ladder, Designed to Sell, Flipping Out, Curb Appeal, The Stagers,* and *Extreme Makeover: Home Edition.* Within the genre of reality TV, these programs dramatized the possibilities of credit-fueled speculation, much as Better Homes demonstration houses had explicated the economic and social potential of mortgage financing in the 1920s. These TV programs reflected and fueled a new culture of homeownership, in which owner-investors saw themselves as commodity speculators using credit to make bets on anticipated inflation and evolving market preferences. Such purchases, renovations, and sales were not only investment strategies but also avocations for aspiring individuals and couples in a society where flexible labor relations and changed attitudes had increased geographical mobility and diminished the sense of rootedness in place and local community.

By liberalizing credit while reducing the regulatory influence of central banks and national governments, global processes have both facilitated homeownership and made it riskier. Since the 1930s a source of "stability, security, and investment," American homeownership has become "a site of uncertainty and risk in which some of the consequences of the changing nature of work and welfare are played out."[29] The recent credit crisis caused the restructuring of Fannie Mae and Freddie Mac,

followed by broader changes in the legal and financial regime through which state and market structure the opportunities and risks of home-ownership and the balance between convention and innovation in house design. It remains to be seen what new cultures of homeownership and housing finance will emerge.

Laura Migliorino, *Egret Street*, 2008, inkjet on canvas

1   On sumptuary regulation, see Alan Hunt, *Governance of the Consuming PassA History of Sumptuary Law* (New York: St. Martin's Press, 1996). For an analysis of the role of sumptuary regulation in the aesthetic of modernist architecture, see Jonathan Massey, "New Necessities: Modernist Aesthetic Discipline," *Perspecta: The Yale Architectural Journal 35* (2004): 112–33.

2   For accounts of the role played by mortgage lending in the credit crisis and broader financial crisis that began in 2007, see Alex Blumberg and Adam Davidson, "The Giant Pool of Money," *This American Life*, episode 355, first aired May 9, 2008; Robert J. Shiller, *The Subprime Solution: How Today's Global Financial Crisis Happened, and What to Do about It* (Princeton, N.J.: Princeton University Press, 2008); and Dan Immergluck, *Foreclosed: High-Risk Lending, Deregulation, and the Undermining of America's Mortgage Market* (Ithaca, N.Y.: Cornell University Press, 2009).

3   Andrew Berman, "'Once a Mortgage, Always a Mortgage': The Use (and Misuse) of Mezzanine Loans and Preferred Equity Investments," *Stanford Journal of Law, Business, and Finance* 11 (Autumn 2005).

4   Department of Commerce, *How to Own Your Home: A Handbook for Prospective Home Owners*, prepared by John M. Gries and James S. Taylor, Division of Building and Housing, Bureau of Standards (Washington, D.C.: U.S. Government Printing Office, 1923), vii. See also Michael Doucet and John Weaver, *Housing the North American City* (Montreal: McGill-Queens University Press, 1991), 252.

5   The characterization of the late nineteenth-century development and financing system in this and the following paragraphs is based primarily on Doucet and Weaver, *Housing the North American City*; and Sam Bass Warner, *Streetcar Suburbs: The Process of Growth in Boston, 1870–1900* (Cambridge, Mass.: Harvard University Press and MIT Press, 1962). For an overview of American single-family house development practices, see Dolores Hayden, *Building Suburbia: Green Fields and Urban Growth, 1820–2000* (New York: Vintage Books, 2003).

6   Thomas C. Hubka and Judith T. Kenny, "The Workers' Cottage in Milwaukee's Polish Community: Housing and the Process of Americanization, 1870–1920," in *People, Power, Places: Perspectives in Vernacular Architecture* 8 (Knoxville: University of Tennessee Press, 2000), 33–52. On the formation and role of savings banks, see R. Daniel Wadhwani, "Citizen Savers: Family Economy, Financial Institutions, and Public Policy in the Nineteenth-Century Northeast," *Enterprise and Society* 5 (2004): 617–23.

7   Warner, "Regulation without Laws," in *Streetcar Suburbs*, 117–52. On the national context of mortgage finance, see Kenneth A. Snowden, "Mortgage Lending and American Urbanization, 1880–1890," *Journal of Economic History* 48 (1988): 273–85; and Lance Davis, "The Investment Market, 1870–1914: The Evolution of a National Market," *Journal of Economic History* 25 (1965): 355–93.

8   Jeffrey M. Hornstein, *A Nation of Realtors: A Cultural History of the Twentieth-Century American Middle Class* (Durham, N.C.: Duke University Press, 2005), 7.

9   My account of Hoover and homeownership campaigns is based primarily on Hornstein, *Nation of Realtors*, 118–55. Regarding BHA, see Janet Hutchison, "The Cure for Domestic Neglect: Better Homes in America, 1922–1935," *Perspectives in Vernacular Architecture* 2 (1986): 168–78; and Karen Altman, "Consuming Ideology: The Better Homes in America Campaign," *Critical Studies in Mass Communication* 7 (1990): 286–307.

10   Better Homes in America, *Guidebook for Better Homes Campaigns in Cities and Towns* (Washington, D.C.: Better Homes in America, 1929), 6, 48.

11   Department of Commerce, *How to Own Your Home*; see also Marc A. Weiss, "Richard T. Ely and the Contribution of Economic Research to National Housing Policy, 1920–1940," *Urban Studies* 26 (1989): 115–26.

12   Hornstein, *Nation of Realtors*, 122–23; Robert S. Lynd and Helen Merrell Lynd, *Middletown: A Study in American Culture* (New York: Harcourt, Brace, and Company, 1929), 104.

13   Better Homes in America, *Guidebook*, 40; Department of Commerce, *How to Own Your Home*, vii.

14   Caroline Bartlett Crane, *Everyman's House* (Garden City, N.Y.: Doubleday Page, 1925), 3.

15   Crane, *Everyman's House*, 149; Weiss, "Richard T. Ely and the Contribution of Economic
        Research to National Housing Policy," 117.

16   Crane, *Everyman's House*, 50.

17   Architects' Small House Service Bureau, Incorporated, *The Movement to Improve Small House
        Architecture* (Minneapolis: The Bureau, n.d. [ca. 1930]).

18   Charles Harris Whitaker, Frederick L. Ackerman, Richard S. Childs, and Edith Elmer Wood,
        "What Is a House?," *American Institute of Architects Journal* 5:2 (1917): 481–85, 541–46, 591–639;
        and "What Is a House?," *American Institute of Architects Journal* 6 (1918): 14–18, 58–67. See also
        Gail Radford, *Modern Housing for America: Policy Struggles in the New Deal Era* (Chicago:
        University of Chicago Press, 1997).

19   Hornstein, *Nation of Realtors*, 119; Robert S. Lynd and Helen Merrell Lynd, *Middletown in
        Transition: A Study in Cultural Conflicts* (New York: Harcourt, Brace, and Company, 1937), 554,
        191.

20   Hornstein, *Nation of Realtors*, 148–50; and Radford, *Modern Housing*, 178.

21   U.S. Federal Housing Administration, *The FHA Story in Summary, 1934–1959* (Washington, D.C.:
        U.S. Government Printing Office, 1959).

22   Hornstein, *Nation of Realtors*, 42–45; Federal Housing Authority, *FHA Homes in Metropolitan
        Districts: Characteristics of Mortgages, Homes, Borrowers under the FHA Plan, 1934–1940*
        (Washington, D.C.: U.S. Government Printing Office, 1942), 5; FHA, *FHA Story in Summary,
        1934–1959*, 15–18.

23   See Ned P. Eichler, T*he Merchant Builders* (Cambridge, Mass.: MIT Press, 1982); and
        Marc A. Weiss, *The Rise of the Community Builders: The American Real Estate Industry and
        Urban Land Planning* (New York: Columbia University Press, 1987).

24   Barbara M. Kelly, *Expanding the American Dream: Building and Rebuilding Levittown* (Albany:
        State University of New York Press, 1993), 77, 87; Federal Housing Administration, *Technical
        Bulletin #2: Modern Design* (Washington, D.C.: U.S. Government Printing Office, 1936); see also
        Keller Easterling, *Organization Space: Landscapes, Highways, and Houses
        in America* (Cambridge, Mass.: MIT Press, 2001), 134, 175–89.

25   Martin Mayer, "Economics of Housing," in *Housing: Symbol, Structure, Site,* ed. Lisa Taylor
        (New York: Cooper-Hewitt Museum and Rizzoli, 1990), 100–101. On redlining and racial
        discrimination, see Kenneth Jackson, *Crabgrass Frontier: The Suburbanization of the United
        States* (Oxford: Oxford University Press, 1987); and Amy Hillier, "Redlining and the Home
        Owners' Loan Corporation," *Journal of Urban History* 29 (May 2003): 394–420.

26   Berman, "'Once a Mortgage, Always a Mortgage," 91–93; and James R. Hagerty, Deborah
        Solomon, and Sudeep Reddy, "Treasury and Fed Pledge Aid for Ailing Mortgage Giants," *Wall
        Street Journal*, July 14, 2008.

27   Blumberg and Davidson, "The Giant Pool of Money." See also U.S. Bureau of the Census,
        American Housing Survey, 2007, www.census.gov/hhes/www/housing/ahs/ahs.html, esp.
        table 3–15; and Guy Stuart, *Discriminating Risk: The U.S. Mortgage Lending Industry in the
        Twentieth Century* (Ithaca, N.Y.: Cornell University Press, 2003).

28   U.S. Bureau of the Census, Characteristics of New Housing Index, 2008,
        http://www.census.gov/const/www/charindex.html.

29   John Doling and Janet Ford, eds., *Globalisation and Home Ownership: Experiences in Eight
        Member States of the European Union* (Delft, the Netherlands: DUP Science, 2003), 7. For a
        broader analysis of contemporary "risk society," see Ulrich Beck, *Risk Society: Towards a New
        Modernity* (London: Sage, 1992); and Beck, *What Is Globalization?* (Cambridge: Polity
        Press, 2000).

Density:
A Conversation about Life, Liberty, and the American Way

Gregg Pasquarelli, Vishaan Chakrabarti, Douglas Gauthier, and Philip Nobel

GREGG PASQUARELLI I'll start with questions. What are the best current ideas about density and infrastructure? Where should the investment go? Is it a zero-sum game?

VISHAAN CHAKRABARTI Well, it's not a zero-sum game, because what has gotten clearer and clearer as the economy has crashed is that cities are in competition with each other primarily for talent. We have to keep creating cool, interesting places in New York City in which people can work and play, in order to keep our competitive advantage. Pivoting to housing, it's amazing to me how you can look at a map of foreclosures in the region, and there are fewer and fewer foreclosures as you get closer to the center of the city. And that's not because it's richer as you get closer to the center; there's more to it than just that. It's the fact that there's actually much more economic resilience with density. The landscape of foreclosure is largely a sprawling landscape. It is not a dense landscape. So this whole idea of what we've created in New York in the last ten years is critical to how successful we've been in protecting ourselves against the economic decline in the last few years.

DOUGLAS GAUTHIER It's almost like you have to put it in terms of Jefferson and Hamilton. It's as though the foreclosures are in a Jeffersonian America—

VC And Hamiltonian America is doing a hell of a lot better.

DG Exactly. We may be claiming him ex post facto. But it seems like Hamiltonian thinking, versus Jeffersonian agrarianism, does lead to that resilience you're talking about. I think, too, that at the time of September 11, we turned a corner, where there was a realization that, if that's the worst thing they can do to us, we can still live in cities. In some ways there was an American competitiveness regarding living in cities then, living densely—like, bring it on. If you didn't hate New York too much, there was a certain amount of pity. And once you had a little bit of pity, you could start to see what was there. This is the outside world looking in on New York as an example of a way of living and thriving with density. But it seemed like kindness became a consensus among Americans elsewhere at that time. They were saying, "Hey, look: It's cool. There's stuff going on there that may not be going on in the suburbs or exurbs." You could also credit *Sex and the City*—

GP Or *Friends*—

DG As part of what has domesticated New York, made dense living familiar and appealing to a much wider group in recent years.

GP I think that idea about Hamilton versus Jefferson—first of all, wasn't it Hamilton who argued that the United States should take on debt? I think it was a big battle appropriate to remember in this time and place. But that idea of economic resilience through density, it's this thing that I always see when I'm out in community boards and I'm talking to people about building projects: there's a fundamental misunderstanding about density. A lot of times you have people go into these neighborhoods and ask, "Are you against gentrification?" Absolutely. "Are you for sustainability?" Absolutely. "Are you for density?" Absolutely not. People are misunderstanding the issue, the equation of density, sustainability, and civic health. It's an economic, it's a political, it's an environmental argument. And they all tie together in this idea of simply living closer together. With that said, the question becomes: What do we as architects have to do to make living densely bearable to Americans today? What are the things we have to do—in cities, in suburbs, in the sprawl? What can we do at the level of the design of a particular building type, of an individual building?

PHILIP NOBEL We could start by pinpointing more exactly what it is that makes people uncomfortable with the idea of density. What is the resistance you find, for instance, in the community boards?

GP Basically, often, "You're ruining my life because there's going to be a shadow on my house."

DG It's like the downzoning of the Lower East Side. Towers like Hotel on Rivington or Bernard Tschumi's Blue can't get built any longer because the zoning has been changed as a result of their construction. And that whole area is underbuilt.

VC The Lower East Side is underbuilt. When we were doing public hearings for the High Line rezoning, a woman who lived in a town house in the West 20s stood up and said, "When these buildings"—and she wasn't even talking about the high buildings in the High Line rezoning; these were maybe buildings that were seven or eight stories tall—"go up, I'm going to be able to see them from my garden." And I said, "Excuse me, ma'am, but as a city official, I cannot let that be my priority. My priority is to help solve the housing crisis in the city, help solve the infrastructure crisis in this city, and help build this city's economy to strengthen the tax base." Right? That's really the problem. And it does go back to Jefferson and Thoreau and a whole cultural milieu in which people believe that their patch of grass is actually more important than the benefits to all that might accrue from living in a dense circumstance. To me that extends beyond New York: there are lots of examples around the country of people living in more density versus less density, and the fact that the latter are more resilient as a consequence.

DG Let's look at the Portland model. Restricting growth to the center worked for a few years. And then everybody who owned property in the outlying sprawl started suing the city government because, basically, their opportunity costs were being taken away. They went from a six zoning, say, to a two. So what Portland did was say, OK, you can exchange it. You can exchange those zoning rights within the urban ring, making the city more dense and the hinterlands less dense. Boulder has a similar rule.

VC Yeah, but I think the problem with those models is that they're based on a regulatory framework, where you then have to do all these weird market mechanisms to adjust for the regulations. I think the name of the game in the future is going to be how you charge people for the negative externalities of their behavior. If you want to drive your obese children to school in a light truck, instead of walking them to school or taking them to school in a fuel-efficient vehicle—

GP Or on public transportation—

VC You need to pay the piper. If you want to live in a 6,000-square-foot McMansion in the exurbs, it shouldn't be illegal; it should just be really, really expensive. That, I think, is where we need to get: where we just price out bad behavior. If you look at, even in these last couple of years, spikes in gas prices relative to increased use of mass transit, there's a Pavlovian response to energy prices. And there needs to be a Pavlovian response on a land-use basis in terms of the housing we create. Because people, I think, will quickly move into much denser circumstances with an increase in energy costs.

DG You're saying it's almost that *ease* has to be taken away. Your gas example is right on—it's a cost that everyone then buys a Prius in response to. But it seems like the critique of the Portland model, or Boulder, or the other places adopting similar regulatory systems, is that it's always telling people what to do, basically taking something away rather than limiting ease in a free-market context.

GP So what's an example of that?

DG That's my question. What do you limit? Do you raise the price of parking? Or simply access from the edge?

VC Driving into Manhattan. You should have to pay a $30 toll to drive one-way into Manhattan.

PN The Port Authority is almost doing that on their own. Some bridge tolls are going up to $14 or $15.

DG Like the London model—$20 to drive downtown.

VC It's still not enough as far as I'm concerned. And there's still the East River bridges, which are really the problem. And then Giuliani removed the commuter tax when he was considering a senatorial bid. We could finance so much infrastructure in this city if we just had the right pricing policy on access to the core.

GP If the people that used it paid for it.

DG It's all about finding the price point.

VC You could do three things, and you would change the landscape of America in terms of housing, in terms of density. You could price for the pollution associated with people's behavior, whether that was gasoline, air-conditioning, or heating big houses. Basically, pricing responsibly for people's energy use. You could drastically reduce or eliminate the mortgage deduction—which I think is actually going to happen step by step as we contemplate deficit reduction. And you could find a new balance in the amount of funding between highways and mass transit. If you just make these politically difficult but mechanically quite simple changes, the whole way we use land in this country changes—for the better.

PN But go back to high-speed rail and this idea of feasibility. Didn't the governor of Florida recently, last year sometime, reject a gift of billions for that state's planned system?

DG He threw away the money.

PN So with that in mind, to pivot from these if not nanny-state then still certainly classic control-model government solutions—the right policy will shape people—isn't there also a way to change *taste*? To make it so, culturally, people actually want these things, want to live in a certain way, and will do it on their own? I'm thinking a little about the explosion of *Dwell*, say. People reading that magazine are much less likely to buy a McMansion and end up hauling their fat kids around in an SUV to a school that's too far away because the land beneath them is being wasted in the service of an outmoded style of living. And that's hundreds of thousands of people now, a cohort that didn't really exist until recently.

VC The problem with influencing taste—

PN Isn't it better to get people to want to do something?

VC That's the *Sex and the City* argument: that by making cities more attractive to the populace, people will want to live in more dense circumstances.

PN Sure. Or even the dense suburbs.

GP It doesn't have to be Manhattan density.

PN There are all those malls being built now in the "town center" model. It's housing above the stores, Jane Jacobs stuff, but it just happens to be like eleven stories of housing and the store is Target.

VC Yeah, I just worry it could end up being the worst of both worlds. The Brookings Institution has been pushing a regionalist agenda, this thing about "walkable urbanism," and they're talking about places like that. And what you find out is that nirvana, in those terms, is Bethesda, Maryland. But you go to Bethesda, and everyone drives everywhere, right? There they really fight hard against density, actually, because the more density you have, the more traffic you get. There isn't enough density to support mass transit.

DG San Francisco is the same way. All those different trains, and it adds up to a mediocre mass-transit system.

VC Right. It's an incredible lie. Everyone drives everywhere.

DG You can't exist without a motor vehicle in San Francisco.

PN Which is crazy, because it's one of a very few contiguously urban areas in the entire country.

VC But look, it has to be done right. The Florida high-speed rail example is a classic. That was a really stupid idea. First of all, it barely cut travel time from what it takes in a car. Second, there are no mass-transit nodes on either end of it. The reason it was in Florida is only because Florida is a purple state. This is a political problem. The density is in the blue states. The blue states need the infrastructure to support that density. But the red states get a disproportionate vote relative to their populations.

GP Because we have two senators from every state.

PN It's also an issue that the less dense red states are the beggar states. The blue states tend to be donor states, giving more to the federal government than they take back in services.

VC Right. The beggar states keep the donor states from building the infrastructure that they could pay for themselves. Am I getting boring and wonky?

DG No. I'm a true believer in your wonkiness. But let's play on the surface for a while. It's consuming, and it's clear, and it's precise, the way you speak. Your lecture to the real estate students at Columbia is the most radical thing they've ever heard. They go in wanting to be you, and then they're like, "Yeah, but he's got some fucked-up politics. He hates the suburb I grew up in!"

PN But suburbs are awful: they waste resources, they make people miserable, and they destroy the land.

GP But besides that, they're great!

VC They should just be superexpensive. That's my theory: not to regulate them out of existence, just to make them really, really expensive to inhabit.

GP Make them pay their real cost.

VC Make them pay the real cost of what they cost society as a whole.

GP Right.

DG But couldn't "superexpensive" influence what is popular? Because if it's superexpensive to live on the outskirts—

PN It'll become aspirational?

DG Exactly.

PN In a way, it's already there. It is superexpensive to heat and furnish a McMansion or to fuel an SUV.

GP But not nearly in line with its real cost.

VC Look—and tell me if this isn't skating on the surface—but it took over twenty years for housing prices after the Depression to correct to precrash values. And I think we're in for a similar ride in this country. To me, that means that a lot of these places that were built in the Vegas desert and outside Phoenix and all of that, they're going to return to desert.

DG The housing studio I'm working on now, there's a project on 149th Street in Harlem, the Dunbar Houses. It's really tight garden apartments at a 2.5 FAR [floor area ratio], which is ridiculous. It was a Rockefeller investment. And it's still suffering from 1929. It has never made it back. It's gone private. It's at about $400 per unit, for these really tight, nice, 800-square-foot two-bedrooms that are subsidized. But 150 of the 600 units are empty, because the owner is trying to get it up to market rate. Now, wouldn't every Columbia graduate—or Syracuse graduate—move up there if they could? But the regulatory context, the rent controls, create this friction.

GP Do we believe that rent control causes the average price of apartments to go up or down?

VC Rent control skews the market.

PN Does it skew the market more than greed?

VC Greed *is* the market. Greed can't skew the market. Greed forms the market.

PN Which is why the market is *bad*.

VC Some people would say there is no market, that it's simply another form of government. To me, rent control is a well-intentioned, very poorly executed idea. So say we all got our dream, and suburbs were really expensive or mowed down by regulations—somehow gone as a viable place for great numbers to inhabit wastefully. The next question is, How do cities become more affordable, more livable, so you don't have huge problems down the line in terms of where people live? Then it's all about construction cost and the fact that new construction delivery in a city like New York is absurdly expensive. If you really want to make housing affordable, then it's really about how to get those costs down. And this is where architects and developers have real common cause.

PN But aren't architects still often paid as a percentage of construction cost?

DG Sometimes. And that's the architect's biggest problem. It's a constant kerfuffle. It sets up an adversarial relationship between the person you're serving and the system, the bottom line. And the AIA [American Institute of Architects] has never solved that. This is your discussion, Gregg, that the AIA should be a development company that puts out competitions for young architects, rather than putting its money into lobbying.

GP And the AIA should negotiate all your contracts. And be a collection agency.

VC Like the mob?

GP It's what's done in a lot of countries: you pay a fee, and you've got a team of lawyers that fight on your behalf. But let's look more at this idea of the cost of things. That leads us to another side of the housing problem. Let's just say that a big thing that's happened in the last decade in New York, through the Bloomberg administration, is this incredible attention to public space, to the quality of buildings, their reflection in public space, the construction of quality infrastructure—that's raised the tax base. The negative side to it is that the city has gotten really expensive, and it starts to force out a lot of the creative minds that made it an attractive place to live and work to begin with. So you can ask, Are we killing ourselves by making the city so nice that all, let's call it, "the talent," can't afford to be here? Then why do you come? I would make the argument that there are now hundreds and hundreds of city square blocks that were, ten years ago, twenty years ago, completely uninhabitable by the creative class. And now they are. Huge swaths of Brooklyn and Queens, Jersey City, Harlem, Inwood. You can go on and on, listing neighborhoods that didn't have the creative class in residence but now do. So I think it has worked, in general, the changes in the city. But the point is, what is the downside? Why is it so important to control construction costs? Why is it so important to have a wide range of income levels blended together?

DG What is the argument for diversity?

GP Yes. What really is the argument for diversity, beyond racial diversity?

VC People keep trying to define it. I mean, you've got prominent architecture critics today who call Manhattan a gated community. It's obscene. It's totally faith-based, as opposed to fact-based. If you really look at the facts, if you look at the cities with which Manhattan, all of New York, competes—London, Hong Kong, Tokyo—

DG We're a bargain.

VC And we have way more socioeconomic diversity than any of those other global capitals. If you go to the Square Mile in London, you cannot swing a cat without hitting an investment banker. I think this is one of the places people go astray when they talk about density and diversity. You know, are they comparing New York to Baltimore? Is that really the apt comparison? Or Portland? I think New York is doing pretty well compared to its true sister cities around the world.

DG It's always an interesting thing when you're learning a city, growing up. You come into New York and it's so wickedly variable, block by block.

PN Right. The *Times* just ran a story this week about the great cultural rift along 97th Street. How many times have they written that article? How has that really changed in our lifetime?

GP It used to be 96th Street. Things *have* changed!

DG But New York really is different—dense and integrated. If you go into the main three square miles of London or Paris, there are people who are poor, but nobody is downwardly mobile poor there.

VC Paris is interesting in that regard. If you go to the Champs-Élysées by day, it's mainly tourists. And then at night, with the sun going down, down comes the guillotine. It totally changes, because all the RER train lines from primarily poor, Muslim neighborhoods on the edge connect under the Champs-Élysées. So it totally transforms: hookahs come out, and the place is completely different. But what's astonishing is how segregated it is. It's like the two cultures never mix. It's dense, it's urban, but socially it's broken.

GP So what's the conclusion?

PN Let's come up with something hopeful, perhaps inspiring.

GP No, seriously, I think what we're talking about are fundamental issues that in today's political climate too often take a backseat. But in fact, how we use the land—how we can use it more efficiently, more fairly, more sustainably—is so primary to all the other issues. If we could solve the issues we've been discussing, or if we could at least engage with them fully and productively as a culture, I think there would be an incredible domino effect on a lot of the other problems the country faces. It's important. This is not about a bunch of New Yorkers discussing the scary suburbs. This is about the fundamental issue of how we're going to live and survive as a culture as resources become more and more scarce. Is that life going to be a decent life for the majority of people living it? What I tried to say before is: What can architects do? We can try to change the government. We can try to change the banking system. We can try to change the tax code. But at the end of the day—I'm already forty-five, I have only X years left to practice— my goal as an architect is to try to make dense living as pleasant as possible.

VC That's great, Gregg. My goal is to amend the Constitution so that foreign-born citizens can become president. Actually, honestly, I think what a lot of our discussion proves is that the modernists largely had it right.

GP The devil was in the details?

PN I was wondering about that when we started talking—how modernist theories on urban development may have contributed to this "I need my light and air," antidensity strain in American thought.

VC They did. In terms of tower-in-the-park thinking, the problem is, it's not dense enough! Most of it would run at a FAR of about 3.4. That's the number for a lot of NYCHA [New York City Housing Authority] housing. It's incredibly low. That's the issue. That's where we fell apart in terms of generating a paradigm that's actually useful in confronting the problems we've been discussing, the problems we face today.

DG Right. The Seward Park towers in Manhattan, for instance, have 2 million feet of FAR that they haven't used, that they could transfer. Penn South has 2.5 million square feet. It's wasted space. But they can't give up those parks, parks that nobody ever uses.

VC They are all evidence of the same landscape obsession that is central to so much post–World War II thinking: loving the machine, and at the same time hating the machine and needing a natural buffer. I think it's critical to the American thought process. And that's where so much goes so wrong.

PN With Jefferson?

GP It was Thoreau.

DG It was Thoreau.

VC It was Thoreau. Thoreau was the bad guy. Thoreau is the enemy.

On Practice
Andrew Bernheimer

Our practice has grown and evolved through self-initiated design projects, motivated by curiosity, ambition, and impatience. Founded in 1998, our company started with design competitions, a conventional method of testing a creative relationship. But convention has not proved expedient or rewarding for those who have not yet turned gray or lost all their hair. We learned this practically: following premiation in a major competition for the plaza at the Phillip Burton Federal Building in San Francisco and the eventual construction of the project, there was a great reversion because of our youth, inexperience, and distance from the East Coast architectural power structure. Despite this major public commission, we were back to the typical tasks of a young, upstart firm: apartments and minor renovations for friends and family. In order to truncate the process of professional development, we resolved to sidestep the conventional career paths for architects. We actively engaged the economic modes of production and the events that precede the design process, those that happen prior to architecture and construction. Four residential projects of differing scales, scopes, and clients exemplify our engagement with alternative or accelerated methods of design and construction that are economic and not simply technological, and that offer a path to creating identifiable architecture.

First, we developed and formed a collaborative team for the design and construction of ten semidetached two-family houses in East New York, Brooklyn. At the time we conceived this project, we were an office of two, working across from each other, literally face-to-face. Our interest in securing a larger-scale project beyond the typical friends-and-family loft was rooted in impatience—impatience with a status quo that held substantial, complex, and impactful work for those who had practiced longer and knew the "right" people. There were no options, really, but to do it ourselves. A search for clever development opportunities led us to explore city-sponsored programs, and we found the New Foundations program, run by the New York City Department of Housing Preservation and Development (HPD). New Foundations offered vacant lots for sale, with primarily developers and builders (or developer builders) competing for these plots. Architects were attached to the projects, as HPD required

Previous: Della Valle Bernheimer, 245 Tenth Avenue, New York, 2011, view from the High Line

Opposite: Della Valle Bernheimer, Glenmore Gardens, Brooklyn, New York, 2006, rear view

both economic pro forma analysis and architectural drawing as part of the request-for-proposal process. But architects were rarely attached as the principal in such deals; they were involved out of sheer necessity. There was no real precedent for a case in which the architect acted as the source of both the financial clout and the design vision. As such, design-focused architects were rarely granted a voice in the process; our profession is stereotypically seen as an impediment to efficient, cost-effective design. In this case, we made a financial and architectural proposal that gave our firm control over the process as both the development and design principals.

Part of our motivation, beyond simply circumventing the delay that awaits young architects trying to procure projects that may have either aesthetic or social impact on cities, was also to collaborate with other talented architects, to create a team of designers that could alter or affect the identity of a small area of the city. Modern row-house construction within New York City's affordable housing typology has typically offered little house-to-house differentiation, and therefore little opportunity for architecture to create a clear sense of identity or individuation. A first home purchase—a milestone in anyone's life—signifies the act of taking stake in a community. In spirit this project engages architecture in a manner similar to that of Weissenhofsiedlung (1927), in Stuttgart, Germany, but in more pragmatic economic terms. It is not an exhibition about a grandiose concept of new architecture but a collection of small-scale ideas magnified through a variety of deployments by several young architects seeking collaboratively to imbue a humble housing type with

dignity. This project thus engages the realms of aesthetics, economics, and politics to address the basic need for affordable housing.

The New Foundations program allows for land generating little or no tax revenue to be transferred to private developers, who must adhere to certain stipulations and standards describing how and what can be built. The program's typical subscribers are developer contractors, firms that can finance, design, and build homes under one imprimatur. We responded to this program—along with Architecture Research Office (ARO), BriggsKnowles A+D, and Lewis.Tsurumaki.Lewis—with the intention of challenging such stereotypes.

Via a charette process, the four firms developed two housing types that mimic the local architectural language: a slab-on-grade three-story structure and a two-story building with subgrade floors and a stoop entry. Simultaneously, we developed a palette of materials to be shared across the houses. Each architecture firm had full latitude in the deployment of these materials to create unique exterior compositions. Standardized details were developed for all houses, and the architects shared these details within their differentiated compositions in order to reduce costs and control the quality and consistency of construction.

In the two buildings designed by Della Valle Bernheimer, we signified difference through either a directional shift in a common material or an explicit change in the type of cladding. In one structure, primary cladding material is recycled aluminum that shifts 90 degrees along the party wall

Opposite: Della Valle Bernheimer, 459 West 18th Street, New York, 2011, setback detail

Above: Della Valle Bernheimer, 459 West 18th Street, New York, 2011, kitchen in one of the units

of two semidetached homes. This simple directional change creates an identifiable difference through light and color transitions. Though the primary material remains consistent over the bulk of the building, the rotation causes the aluminum to appear dark or light, gray or white, depending on the time of day and type of light. In a second house, a cedar box embeds itself within a corrugated aluminum shell at the second floor. This wooden object distinguishes the homeowner's territory from the first-floor rental unit.

The second project we completed as principals of both design and development is a residential building at 459 West 18th Street in West Chelsea, Manhattan. The primary architectural expression for this building involves two interlocking volumes that articulate the restrictions and requirements of the building's zoning district. Our office continually views these restrictions as challenges and opportunities; where some designers may feel constrained by the rules, our studio looks at them as compositional and informative, opportunities for design rather than impediments to creativity. On an experiential level, the design intention was to construct a solid building that would give occupants a panoramic connection to the city. We also sought to avoid fabricating a normative piece of modern architecture, the glass box. Simultaneously, we examined the modern precedent of "colorless" architecture made from metal and glass, materials that in primary form impart no color or tonal gradients to the artifice they define. Our first studies were of binary conditions, or architecture made from opposites. Several iterations of orthogonal blocks were composed, with the final form assuming the shape of the idealized zoning diagram.

While many new buildings express visual connectivity to the city through ubiquitous expanses of transparent surfaces—for example, a new building on an adjacent property is composed of folded planes of floor-to-ceiling curtain-wall glass—our design posits that a solid, totemic object can be equally revealing. Whereas many buildings express their openness literally, the facade of 459 West 18th Street presents swatches of voids. Extruded aluminum collars hold enormous expanses of unbroken, seamless glass. In this way, the window becomes a minimal yet severe vitrine that is mostly invisible but forces spatial containment. The monumental openings, measuring as much as 8 by 18 feet, take the background of the city and place it at the forefront of one's experience. The windows are detailed with this minimalist aesthetic in mind. Mullions are only two inches thick, and the frame for the vent is nested within the mullion to conceal its operating mechanisms. All hardware disappears, while interruptions within glass expanses are kept to a minimum. The building is thus articulated as a pair of linked or nested dualities: solid and void, black and white.

Another project in Chelsea, 245 Tenth Avenue, is a 54,000-square-foot
residential tower containing nineteen apartments and two art galleries.
Sited on an odd-shaped lot at the corner of 24th Street and 10th Avenue,
the building is predominantly party wall. Typically these walls are left blank,
mute. Through a redeployment of square footage to the upper reaches
of the building (all within the allowed zoning envelope), we designed
a billowing shape meant to evoke the clouds of steam from the trains
that used to travel along the High Line tracks, adjacent to the site. This
displacement of square footage made it affordable to surface the party
walls in a material that went beyond the material typically used for such
a purpose. We used the real estate to activate and facilitate the design
process; the appearance of the building is the direct result of an ability
to observe the project as more than just a series of surfaces and shapes,
to see the architectural process as intertwined with the existing code
and the market economy.

Our design studies were based on the shapes of clouds emanating from
the smokestacks of steam trains. Dissipating into the sky, these clouds
tended to have dark, thick tones at their base and would billow, dissolve,
and lighten into the sky. Their vaporous, tonal metamorphoses inform
both the architectural form of the building and the texture of its skin
through embossing. To replicate the phenomenon of clouds, we made
several digital studies of a steam-engine cloud and isolated a small area
depicting the gradient from black to white. This area was then pixelated
and overlaid onto the facade in accordance with a variety of contextual
conditions pertaining to privacy, view, and light. Five types of pixels were
designed and then transformed from dots to protruding diamonds in
order to capture light. Custom dyes for a computer-numerical-control
(CNC) turret punch (like a large-scale typewriter) were manufactured.
As 2-by-4-foot panels run through the machine, a digital drawing instructs
it to punch each piece of stainless steel with a pattern of diamonds,
reimaging and transposing the cloud across the facade of the building.
These raised diamonds catch light differently throughout the day and
year; though fixed materially, each facade is a mutable surface. Ornament
is made inextricable from architecture, justifying its presence on both
aesthetic and economic levels.

Lastly, and at a far smaller (though perhaps far more important) scale,
we completed the design for R-House, a full collaboration with ARO.
A winning entry in Syracuse University's From the Ground Up competition,
R-House is an effort in creating a durable model for sustainable architecture. In this case, sustainable does not refer simplistically to a zenergy

(though the house does address these issues sensitively). Rather, sustainability is thought of in terms of injecting lasting identity and architectural presence into a neighborhood in need of regeneration, and in terms of creating an architecture that is healthy both physically and economically. Throughout the collaboration, our firms focused on the viability of this house as an economic generator, as a physically healthy space, and as a flexible container for a wide variety of family units.

R-House is designed as a Passivhaus, meeting the stringent German standards for this technology. The house will use 90 percent less energy than a typical residence and can be heated with the amount of energy used to run a hair dryer. The house incorporates a superinsulated envelope that reduces the energy demands of the structure while raising air and light quality, creating what is quite literally a healthier environment. With a gently altered form derived from the standard icon of gabled roof structures, we reimagined familiar house design, identifying this house as something new and different within an established community. Its form is simple and compact, encompassing only 1,100 square feet.

R-House's adaptability to different needs over time is fundamental to its sustainability. The base plan is designed to grow from a two-bedroom

house to a three- or four-bedroom house simply by extending the second floor over a double-height living space. This void can be filled and the entry sequestered, allowing for a separate rental unit to further enhance the economic viability of the home. Based on the Syracuse housing market for the Near Westside neighborhood, this additional rental income would provide financial sustainability for its owner. It was vital to offer an effective subsidy to the homeowner's expenses; the concept of sustainability extended beyond the material and into the community.

For our firm, practicing architecture requires a great resilience and durability. It requires entrepreneurship and imagination. Housing, in particular, offers us the opportunity to make projects happen on our own. It offers an opportunity to locate our identity within our own designs. Most important, it offers those living in our designs the opportunity to identify themselves.

Opposite: Della Valle Bernheimer with Architecture Research Office, R-House, Syracuse, New York, 2011, street view

Above: Della Valle Bernheimer with Architecture Research Office, R-House, Syracuse, New York, 2011, interior

High-Rise

56 Leonard Street   New York, New York

Herzog & de Meuron
Square feet: 480,000
Completion date: planned for 2013

Above: Plan

Above, right: Rendering of the
entrance, with a sculpture by
Anish Kapoor

Opposite: Rendering of the
tower in context

Previous: Studio Gang Architects,
Aqua Tower, Chicago, Illinois, 2010,
view of the undulating facade

The ambition of 56 Leonard Street is to achieve, despite the tower's size, a personalized, perhaps even intimate, character. The project is conceived as a stack of individual houses, each of which is unique and identifiable within the overall structure.

Floor slabs were shifted and varied to create corners, cantilevers, and balconies—all strategies for providing different features in each apartment. The base of the tower reacts to the scale and conditions of the street, while the top staggers and undulates to merge with the sky. The middle levels, like the shaft of a column, are more controlled and subtle.

The tower, exceptionally tall and slender given its relatively small footprint, shows its bones: exposed horizontal concrete slabs register the floor-by-floor stacking, and exposed concrete columns on the interior allow residents to experience the scale of the structural forces at work. The system of staggering and setbacks is further animated through operable windows in every second or third facade unit, an unusual feature for high-rise buildings.

550 St. Clair

Chicago, Illinois

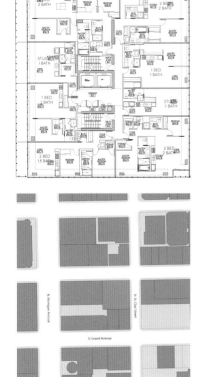

Brininstool + Lynch
Square feet: 223,800
Completion date: 2008

Above: Plan

Above, right: Kitchen and
dining area of a typical unit

Opposite: Street view from
Michigan Avenue

550 St. Clair is a multiresidential development with a level of design detail typical of custom single-family homes. The forms, systems, and materials were selected to provide both openness and privacy, as well as flexibility of use and functionality.

The residential tower rises as a single eighteen-story volume enclosed by sheer planes of window glass on the north, east, and south elevations and relieved at the corners by inset balconies with translucent glazing. The floor-to-floor windows incorporate operable units set above eye level. Sliding doors open onto projected terraces on the west side, creating six-foot openings. A perimeter soffit contains a four-pipe horizontal system to optimize thermal comfort while providing a source of ambient lighting and space for integrated window treatments.

Floors two through seven contain a garage that is sheathed in a woven stainless-steel scrim and suspended between translucent backlit glazing at the ground-level retail spaces and at the eighth-floor fitness facility.

Macallen Building   Boston, Massachusetts

Office dA with Burt Hill
Square feet: 350,000
Completion date: 2007

Above: Plan

Above, right: Kitchen and
dining area of one of the
condominium units

Opposite: Street view
showing the garage

A pivotal project in the urban revitalization of South Boston, the Macallen Building occupies a transitional site that mediates between highway off-ramps, an old residential fabric, and an industrial zone. The design addresses two different scales and the various conditions of the surrounding area by creating private spaces that relate to the public sphere through material choice and the building's facade.

On the western end, the design responds to the highway with a curtain wall that provides panoramic views from inside the building. On the eastern end, the brickwork mirrors that of the residential building fabric, extending the logic of the adjacent storefront and pedestrian-scale elements. On the north and south facades, bronzed aluminum panels reflect the industrial component of the neighborhood and express the organization of the building's structural system. In addition, the Macallen Building was designed from the ground up to take advantage of green construction techniques and materials, and it is the first LEED-certified building of its type in Boston.

Culver House

Chicago, Illinois

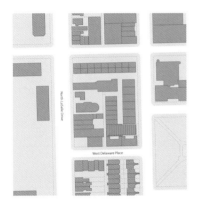

Dirk Denison Architects
Square feet: 30,375
Unbuilt

Above, right: Rendering of roof
terraces and balconies

Opposite, top: Rendering of
the main living space in one unit

Opposite, bottom: Plan

Culver House demonstrates a green development initiative in an urban
context. The building is planned as a sustainable mixed-use development:
one commercial space occupies the ground floor, and eight residences
populate the second through sixth floors. Designed to provide generous
and diverse space for living and working, the building is configured with
varied plans and sections.

The ultimate goal of Culver House is to push the envelope of green
design strategies in a private mixed-use project, in hopes of setting
a higher standard for future developments throughout the city and region.
The project seeks to expand the high-profile environmentally conscious
endeavors of the city government into the private sector, offering publi-
cized city initiatives like green roofs and optimized energy performance
as amenities for the building's residents.

The project rethinks an underutilized site in a vibrant area of the city
directly across from historic Washington Square Park. It seeks to employ
existing infrastructure; a small warehouse building on the site is kept
largely intact and reused, while the new portion of the building is built
in front of and above it.

High Line 519 — New York, New York

Lindy Roy/Roy Co.
Square feet: 18,600
Completion date: 2007

Above, right: Detail of the front
facade system

Opposite, top: Plan

Opposite, bottom: Street view

High Line 519 is an eleven-story residential condominium building adjacent to the High Line park at West 23rd Street in Manhattan. The design process began with the expressed desire to register the individual identity of each floor-through apartment on the north and south facades.

The building volume prescribed by the zoning envelope for this 25-foot-wide sliver lot presented a challenge. The narrow but tall dimensions required a disproportionate percentage of the construction budget to address the lateral stability of the building. Given the relatively small floor plates, the design process had to be approached strategically.

Design was focused on the "free space" defined by New York City regulations that allow decorative architectural features to project several inches beyond the street-facing lot line. A series of 4-inch-deep balustrades skim the building's front facade, linking the staggered French doors of each successive apartment. On the rear, similar shapes project out as balcony balustrades. A honeycomb-embossed, perforated stainless-steel material used to line washing-machine drums was selected for both its industrial origins and its refined, dynamic effect.

HL23

New York, New York

Neil M. Denari Architects, Inc. (NMDA)
Square feet: 38,750
Completion date: 2011

Above: Main entrance

Above, right: Living area of a typical unit

Opposite: View of the tower from
the High Line

HL23 is a fourteen-story condominium tower that was constructed on a very compact site adjacent to the High Line park at West 23rd Street in New York's Chelsea neighborhood. With a custom nonspandrel curtain wall on the south and north facades, and a 3-D stainless-steel panel facade on the east facing the High Line, the building's geometry is driven by challenges to the site's zoning envelope and by the architects' interest in achieving complexity through simple tectonic operations.

Each floor consists of one residential unit, except for the second and thirteenth floors, which are duplex units. Above the fourth floor, the structure projects outward, creating an undulating facade that cantilevers over the High Line. The building's south facade features a structural diagonal that helps the cantilevered floors "hang" from the interior columns.

The building is designed as a complex prism whose proportions, angles, and profiles continue to shift as one walks past it on the High Line. In this sense, although HL23 is a private building, it participates in the public experience of the park.

Aqua Tower   Chicago, Illinois

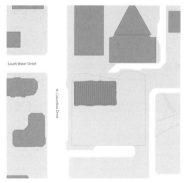

South Water Street

N. Columbus Drive

Studio Gang Architects
Square feet: 1,900,000
Completion date: 2010

Above: Exterior balconies

Above, right: View of the tower
in context

Aqua Tower was shaped by an organic, site-specific design process. Rather than start with the goal of creating an icon, the architects let the climate and views shape the building, recognizing the interconnectedness of the building and its environment.

This eighty-two-story, mixed-use high-rise includes a hotel, apartments, condominiums, offices, and parking. Among the building's notable features is the green roof terrace atop its plinth—at 80,000 square feet, one of Chicago's largest—which contains an outdoor pool, a running track, gardens, fire pits, and a yoga terrace.

A series of contours defined by outdoor terraces extends away from the face of the building structure to provide views between neighboring buildings. These outdoor terraces, cantilevered as much as twelve feet, differ in shape from floor to floor based on criteria such as the view, solar shading, and the size and type of dwelling. When viewed together, the terraces make the building appear to undulate, an effect that is highly sculptural but also rooted in function.

459 West 18th Street

New York, New York

Della Valle Bernheimer acted as both architect and developer of this residential project located between two vibrant and evolving neighborhoods on the west side of Manhattan, the Meatpacking District and Chelsea.

On the edge of what was once the shoreline of Manhattan, this boldly designed mixed-use condominium project appears resolutely within its context. Though the exterior of the tower is severe in mass and profile, its interiors are muted and carefully detailed. The building envelope is made of composite panels and white and clear glass. Fenestration punctures through the building mass are expressed as extruded collars. In an effort to blur the delineation between interior and exterior, massive expanses of glass were used to add a cinematic quality and frame views of the city and the river a block away. Interior details and materials achieve an understated, serene quality that is in marked contrast to the rigorous building exterior and the feel of the neighborhood.

Della Valle Bernheimer
Square feet: 29,700
Completion date: 2009

Above: Interior of one of the units

Above, left: View of the building, midblock at left, from the High Line

40 Bond

New York, New York

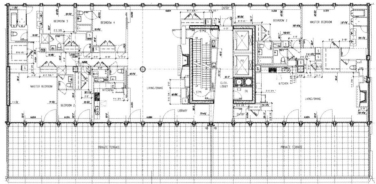

Herzog & de Meuron
Square feet: 83,200
Completion date: 2007

Above, right: Typical upper-floor plan

Opposite, clockwise from top left: view
of the building from Bond Street; detail
of the front facade; the main living space
in one unit

The site, which occupies five typically narrow New York lots, is located on Bond Street, a relatively wide cobblestone street in the heart of NoHo. It is embedded among brownstones, warehouses, and lofts, which vary significantly in scale and proportion.

The five town houses reintroduce the scale of the original lots. Each has a recessed entrance porch across its street frontage and a garden to the rear. The porch is separated from the street by a cast-aluminum gate, which acts as a physical barrier as well as a visual screen. The narrow, double-height entrance lobby for the condominiums connects the street with a small communal garden at the back.

The apartment block is stacked above the town houses and forms a bracket across the site. Its design is a reinvention of the cast-iron building type found throughout the area. The structure of the building follows the grid of the large floor-to-ceiling window bays, introducing depth to the exterior facade and liberating the interior from freestanding columns. Wrapped over the structure are gently curved glass covers, which act as a continuation of the windowpanes.

Jack London Tower

Oakland, California

Stanley Saitowitz/Natoma Architects
Square feet: 437,900
Unbuilt

Right: Rendering of street view

Jack London Tower folds up into the air from a podium that tracks the height of the neighboring buildings along the Embarcadero. Each fold creates a void as it climbs the forty-one stories to the top. These voids serve as common outdoor gardens for the residents—generous vertical parks with trees and greenery.

The low-slung podium building contains parking, a gym with an infinity pool, and glass storefronts that wrap the corner of Broadway. The tower residences float above the podium and are entered through a tall, vertical atrium lobby with a glass roof, a giant volume open to the sky.

The skin of the tower is a shear wall, perforated with variegated windows that provide panoramic views of the San Francisco Bay. A shear core contains the vertical distribution and circulation spaces. Wrapping the core is a bar of services for the units, with open habitable spaces around the perimeter beyond. All units are open and flexible.

New Carver Apartments

Los Angeles, California

Michael Maltzan Architecture
Square feet: 53,000
Completion date: 2009

Clockwise from top left: street view;
corridor looking onto the atrium;
aerial view of the building adjacent
to the freeway; view up through
the atrium

Located just south of the rapidly growing downtown area of Los Angeles and immediately adjacent to Interstate 10, the New Carver Apartments explore how architecture can create new possibilities for dramatically underserved populations and for the city as a whole.

Situated nearly a mile from the heart of Skid Row, the project includes ninety-seven units that provide permanent housing for the formerly homeless, building a place for support and individual growth in the face of the city's chronic homeless problem. The project aims not only to construct a new optimism for public space and public housing in Los Angeles, but also to form an armature for change through the architectural program, organization, and form. By incorporating communal spaces—kitchens, dining areas, gathering spaces, and gardens—into the building's raised form, as well as medical and social-service support facilities into the plinth beneath, the project allows its residents to reconnect with each other as well as the larger city beyond.

Living
Arrangements
Julie
Eizenberg

By 2030, there will be 94 million more people in the U.S. than there were in 2000. And all of these people need somewhere to live, work and shop. Most of this population will live in urban areas—housing units will get smaller, more square footage will be built on smaller sites, there will be less room for cars and communities will have to make some tough choices. But in the end, although the change may be difficult and it may cost more to build on less space, there are definite benefits in terms of a sustained urban lifestyle.

—"A Plan for Tomorrow: Creating Stronger and Healthier Communities Today," Urban Land Institute, May 3, 2006

An exhibition called "Living Arrangements" at the Syracuse University School of Architecture in 2007 documented a variety of our [Koning Eizenberg Architecture's] housing work—some built, some not yet built. The projects were assembled as background for the simultaneous housing studio and provided reference on density and diversity within the building type. The students were examining how the adaptive reuse of a 200,000-square-foot warehouse and adjacent parcel might be revived by an inventive approach to building a mixed-use neighborhood with a core of housing, augmented by community and commercial uses.

Several years later it seems fitting to return to our reference projects (and projects initiated since) and their broad building categories to frame observations on the recent history of the American house and the speed of its change. What emerges is a series of short stories that traces a variety of influences, from sustainability, media, and lifestyle choices to changes in regulations and a boom-and-bust economy. The Urban Land Institute, quoted in the excerpt above, was right that change was imminent and necessary, but I think it underestimated the speed of acceptance and implementation.

Affordable Family: Harold Way

Throughout the 1980s and '90s, and even into the new millennium, the task for architects working in affordable housing was to demonstrate that while

Previous: Koning Eizenberg Architecture, The Standard, Downtown LA, Los Angeles, 2002, view from Flower Street

Opposite: Student design from the Seinfeld Studio, 2007, "Syracuse Mind Body Soul" by Christine McMahan and Eric Zahn

limited budgets might be a constraint, the building type was rich in architectural possibilities that could strengthen community and improve the quality
of daily life. In short, it really does matter how it feels to come home.

The Harold Way housing, completed in 2003 in Los Angeles, provides
a good example. It comprises 51 one-, two-, and three-bedroom units
over subterranean parking. The large units are organized as stacked town
houses, which not only breaks the pancake scale and unrelenting circulation of traditional apartments, but also allows more units to take advantage
of required side yards for generous private outdoor space. Every design
strategy was selected to improve amenities, reinforce opportunities for
social interaction, use resources responsibly, and create a quiet beauty.

In those years the megahousing "projects" of the 1960s, like those on the
South Side of Chicago, loomed large. It is a tough perception to shift, and
although most affordable housing in Los Angeles in the 1980s was generally being delivered through neighborhood-based nonprofit development
companies on small infill sites (from six to one hundred units), communities were anxious. It took some subtlety to integrate affordable housing into
neighborhoods that were still suspicious of the projects. In fact, we were
often asked to make affordable housing look like what was being built in
the market-rate sector. To us, market-rate housing at the time was char-
acterized by expedient, fake traditionalism and set such a low bar that
matching it seemed pointless.

As the new millennium progressed, nonprofits finally built a critical
mass of successful contemporary housing projects, and the sustainability
movement expanded expectations of what housing should look like,
legitimizing thin buildings that cross ventilate (and minimize air-conditioning
use) and validating the value of landscaped common space that was
considered so unusual just a few years earlier. Progressive affordable-
housing developers, like Community Corporation of Santa Monica and Skid
Row Housing Trust in Los Angeles, sponsored and supported demonstrably
sustainable and stylistically ambitious projects, like the Tahiti Housing
Complex by Daly Genik Architects or Step Up on Fifth by Pugh + Scarpa.
Such projects not only served communities and residents well, but also
excited philanthropists. Maybe they were inspired by celebrity efforts like
Brad Pitt's post-Katrina Make It Right foundation work in the Lower Ninth
Ward (ca. 2007).

In the current recession, tax credits and redevelopment funds (core
funding sources for affordable housing) are harder to come by, certainly

Koning Eizenberg Architecture, The Standard, Downtown LA, Los Angeles, 2002, historic entrance on Flower Street

in California. At the same time, lessons learned about the value of design have held. Many foundations and independent philanthropists who support housing are now looking at sustainability and design as part of their investment evaluation. Enterprise Community Partners, a significant housing funder, has started the Affordable Housing Design Leadership Institute, which works to educate affordable-housing developers about the power of design for their communities.[1] Perceptions have changed: we have demonstrated that there is value in design, and lessons from the progressive developers and their architects are influencing the institutional structure of housing.

Short-Term Hotel: The Standard, Downtown LA

Hotels, like all housing, provide a place to lay one's head at night but are too often considered peripheral to building community. Although cities welcome the bed tax, many are not so welcoming to the guests, categorizing them as outsiders with needs that are completely different from, if not incompatible with, those of local residents. I am not sure why; out-of-towners enjoy a coffee or meal at a local cafe and a walk around the neighborhood as much as the rest of us. The rise of the boutique hotel (which offers a combination of design and location) over the last decade validates that observation. More often than not, conventional hotels are sited away from neighborhoods (think of major hotel chains like Hilton or Residence Inn), so no demands are made on them to be good neighbors—and so, in turn, they are not.

Above: Koning Eizenberg
Architecture, AMP Lofts,
Los Angeles, rendering of
bird's-eye view

Opposite: Koning Eizenberg
Architecture, AMP Lofts,
Los Angeles, rendering
of courtyard

But there are exceptions. The Standard, Downtown LA is an example
of a hotel that is not just a good neighbor but also a catalyst for building
neighborhood. It is not such an unusual occurrence these days, but in 2002
the regeneration sparked by the Standard was groundbreaking.

The hotel took over a historic 1950s office building that had been vacant
for years and offered a rooftop bar and pool (surprisingly rare in downtown at that time), with a great view, lounges, and a coffee shop. It quickly
drew both savvy travelers and party-loving Angelenos in large numbers,
and it was one of the few bright spots in a largely deserted downtown
office scene with many vacant buildings. The hotel's immediate success
was noticed by developers who were cautiously looking to capitalize on
recent changes in the city's planning code that incentivized adaptive-
reuse development. Within five years of the opening of the Standard,
there were over 8,500 units of new housing in the vicinity.[2] Most were
commercial building conversions, and some were built new. In 2007 the
first supermarket was built downtown, providing a clear indicator that
urban living had finally taken hold in the area.[3]

The burgeoning aesthetic of the new generation of boutique hotels like
the Standard also raised design aspirations in the market-rate multiunit
housing sector and influenced the design of new projects built in Los
Angeles and elsewhere. The boutique hotel's success and cachet revived
interest in sophisticated and adventurous design, and housing developers
began to invest in common spaces like pools and lounges as not just

"check-the-box" amenities but as design highlights. This was definitely the case on projects we worked on. Some housing even offered a branded, high-style hotel aesthetic. Such was the case with the Philippe Starck brand expressed in Ian Schrager hotels (the Mondrian and the Delano, to name a few), and then with Starck-branded condominium buildings around the world, like the Gramercy Starck in New York. The danger in equating hotel style with housing style is how quickly design taste changes. Whereas it is not uncommon to change and update a hotel's style every few years, multiunit housing is structured to keep its identity relevant over the longer term. In high-style housing the line between adventurous design and fashion victim is very fine.

The contribution of hotel design to strengthening urban communities and influencing the actual design of multiunit housing should not be underestimated. The crossover seems unexpected but really makes sense when one thinks about the similarities of program.

Industrial Light: AMP Lofts

The AMP Lofts will probably never be built. They should have been, but the project fell victim to a quickly changing political context and then bad economic timing. The excitement of the revival of downtown Los Angeles and surrounding neighborhoods was in full swing in 2004 when we were approached to develop a concept design and entitlement package for the AMP Lofts, located in an industrial zone just south of downtown and only a few blocks from the Los Angeles River. The automotive-parts business that had occupied the 2.3-acre site had migrated outside the region a few years earlier, and the owners were interested in promoting joint artist-in-residence live/work units and mixed-use development. They were inspired by other creative live/work projects being developed in a neighborhood made up of underutilized industrial warehouses and manu-facturing facilities that no longer suited their original purpose.

The repurposing of industrial land on a case-by-case basis was progressing at quite a pace following adaptive reuse ordinances that were enacted in the late 1990s and the early years of the twenty-first century, and it offered significant incentives to developers in a booming market.[4] The site's zoning as M3 heavy industrial, which permitted junkyards and scrap metal and equipment storage, still applied, though it was generally recognized that the industrial development of the district was incompat-ible with the upgrades necessary to expand the existing industry.

The AMP Lofts project proposed around 180 units of new live/work housing on an essentially vacant lot and included retail and open spaces that would significantly improve the walkability and street presence of the neighborhood. The AMP Lofts would have provided the largest new green space within any loft development downtown and could have begun to mitigate the negative impacts of past industrial uses. The project took into account the evolving Los Angeles River Master Plan and proposed to help achieve the objective of river revitalization by bringing housing to an area where residents might enjoy the benefits of the emerging green and recreational spaces encouraged by the master plan.

As we were honing the character of the development to suit its industrial context, however, the amount, location, and definition of industrial real estate were being hotly debated and becoming highly politicized. While some found value in maintaining industrial uses, plans to improve the Los Angeles River suggested that industrial uses were contrary to the master plan in the long run, and hopes for the changing nature of the neighborhood encouraged by adaptive reuse ordinances made industrial uses obsolete.

In 2005 the zone was designated an employment protection district by the city's new Industrial Land Use Policy and was required to retain exclusively industrial uses regardless of conflicting plans for the river and on-the-boards housing projects.[5] With backing from the city council, the project was approved despite these restrictions in 2009, but by the time the dust settled, the real estate bubble had burst and the economy had taken a nosedive. After lengthy and well-publicized battles for entitlement, the AMP Lofts simply could not overcome bad timing. Today the site still stands mostly empty, and the owner is trying to sell the property and entitlements to a housing developer.

Koning Eizenberg Architecture, AMP Lofts, Los Angeles, rendering of street view

Mixed Use: Hancock Lofts

One of the most significant lifestyle changes that has occurred over the last fifteen years is the American public's embrace of higher-density, mixed-use urban living. I knew this style would have long-term traction when communities like Brea, deep in Orange County, started building new town centers with movie theaters and multiunit housing above retail in the late 1980s and early 1990s.[6] It was a clear sign that urban living had become a generally accepted lifestyle choice, not just a big-city necessity. Nevertheless, it seemed the

Above: Koning Eizenberg
Architecture, Hancock Lofts, Santa
Monica, California, 2010, street view
of south facade

Opposite: Koning Eizenberg
Architecture, Hancock Lofts, Santa
Monica, California, 2010, loft interior

trend lost steam. In 2004, as we were completing schematic design on the Hancock housing, a mixed-use project in West Hollywood, the story of mixed use still seemed novel in the general development community and even in architecture schools, where I often presented the project.

The Hancock Lofts were a long time in the making; starting with a public/private partnership initiated in 2000, construction was not completed until 2010. The project was designed through an extended public process to determine the acceptable balance between public parking, retail, and housing height and density. Four stories was the maximum height this progressive community was willing to accept, although the project could easily have been a few stories taller without affecting the character of the street. Even for early adopters of sustainable thinking, it was, and still remains, difficult for progressive communities like West Hollywood to buy the relationship between sustainability and optimizing height and density. While local residents were eager for us to outline our sustainable design strategies and renewable-resource material choices, they were unwilling to add a floor level. The community appreciated the value of making active streets and was supportive of the team's efforts not only to line the boulevard with stores but also to hide the parking on the side street with ground-level courtyard units, but it could not make the connection between sustainable, walkable streets and higher-density building.

Looking back, parking is still the elephant in the room. The project was initiated by the city to meet a parking shortage for local businesses, and approximately two parking spaces were required for every unit of housing. We know now, and maybe were not willing to admit then, that easy parking encourages car use. But consciousness of the role of parking in making livable urban communities is rippling through cities. Some West Coast cities like San Francisco now severely restrict rather than encourage parking, and even Los Angeles is reviewing its parking requirements. There is also much talk among transportation planners about the idea of unbundling parking from development so that parking spaces are made available separately from the real estate itself. This strategy acknowledges that parking comes at a cost (structured parking actually costs around $17,000 per stall to build) and assigns it as a premium.[7] The strategy also allows more flexible use allocation in the hope that over time—and with sufficient density, active streets, good public transportation, and encouragement of bicycle and flex car programs—the need for car ownership, even in the Los Angeles area, will decline.

Adaptive Reuse: Century Building, Pittsburgh

Bringing a building back to life is satisfying, but given that times have changed, the intended uses of the building may be different and the perception of what is historically appropriate is always open to interpretation.

The adaptive reuse of the twelve-story, 68,000-square-foot historic Century Building transformed a decaying, largely vacant commercial building into sixty-one mixed-income apartments above two office floors and an existing ground-floor restaurant. Coincidentally, the renovation was completed exactly one hundred years after the Century Building first opened its doors. In the interim, Rust Belt cities had risen and fallen. The lucky ones, like Pittsburgh, are finally coming back to life, this time as mixed-use "livable cities" rather than commercial and manufacturing centers.[8] These cities, with their large inventory of historic buildings, benefited from preservation regulations enacted in the 1990s and the early years of the twenty-first century that arrested the rate of demolition of distinctive historic buildings, and from tax credits that incentivized restoration and reuse.

The Century had a beautiful street elevation in need of repair and a narrow footprint that worked well for housing once windows were added to the predominantly blank side-yard elevations, which are sometimes called blind facades. Had history played out as anticipated, the Century Building's blind facade would have been hidden by neighboring structures rather than fully exposed as was the case now, with one facade serving as backdrop to a plaza and the other fronting a wide public-parking easement. Adding windows to these walls seemed like an opportunity to add contemporary vitality to banal facades that were inadvertently emphasized and always thought of as disassociated from the key street facade. Interestingly, historic preservation guidelines did not require replacement of the dingy brown-tinted glazing on the street facade (probably added in the 1970s) with clear glass (as was done). But they did impose stringent requirements on the design of the new blind-facade window size, proportion, and placement to reflect a bygone era rather than acknowledge a change in lifestyle in downtown Pittsburgh that no one could have anticipated in 1907.

Pittsburgh is where the sustainability movement, through the U.S. Green Building Council, developed the Leadership in Energy and Environmental Design (LEED) program in 1998, which has become a benchmark sustainability metric and has changed expectations for how buildings should measure up socially and environmentally, and relative to responsible energy use. The Century achieved LEED Gold certification and showcases features that warrant further detailed description: adaptive reuse, the commuter bicycle center, and a mixed-income building program.

Adaptive reuse is an obvious and important sustainable strategy. Work still needs to be done to align common-sense sustainability with historic

guidelines that restrict aesthetics as well as mandate visible and not-so-visible material choices, but the benefits of legacy and continuity cannot be overestimated. The bicycle commuter center offers forty-nine secure bike spaces and addresses livability and responsible use of resources through alternative mobility. It leverages small opportunities—an unused easement, two recycled shipping containers, and some paint—to advertise the program and animate the street.

Most significant, the Century Building's mixed-income housing program (40 percent affordable housing) provides a successful prototype to dispel the fears of real estate industry naysayers who insist that different income groups will not mix. The Century offered the first new affordable housing downtown and the first mixed-income housing in the region. Even before completion, interest in both the affordable and market-rate units was overwhelming; there were more than one thousand names on the opening waiting list. The Century continues at full occupancy, housing the elderly, young couples, and the disabled in lofts and one- and two-bedroom units.

The Century is an illustrative case study of ongoing efforts in adaptive reuse, highlighting some of its contradictions and also expanding the possibilities for building community.

Above, left and right: Koning Eizenberg Architecture, Century Building, Pittsburgh, Pennsylvania, 2010, exterior facade and loft interior

Lofts: Electric Art Block

Even in 1991, when the Electric Art Block lofts were built, the idea of the live/work loft was not new. In Los Angeles, Frank Gehry and Chuck Arnoldi had built the Indiana lofts for Dennis Hopper, and in New York the SoHo art scene and expansive bohemian live/work lifestyle was well established and often imitated. Gehry and Arnoldi's Indiana lofts were innovative because they provided raw, high-ceilinged spaces from scratch rather than as an adaptive reuse in the SoHo style. The Electric Art Block lofts were similarly built from the ground up, but for a developer, not an owner-user, and were the harbinger of a trend in new housing development.

The Electric Art Block was one of the first new developments to take advantage of artist-in-residence permits in Los Angeles that allowed housing to be built in industrial/commercial zones, much of which included a large amount of underutilized buildings and real estate. The planning initiative provided an early inroad into decompartmental-izing conventional twentieth-century zoning, which separated uses and undermined architects' ability to provide the Jane Jacobs–esque quality of life that the planning community suddenly realized was missing. Architects, planners, and communities were slowly realizing that maybe it was all right for workplace and housing to be side by side or even mixed up.

While artists needed to purchase an artist's license from the city to qualify for occupancy, developers benefited from relaxed interpretations of the codes for the configuration of kitchens and bedrooms and number of parking spaces. Not everyone who moved in was a practicing artist (or even worked from home); many just wanted the ambience of the creative environment offered by artist-in-residence types of lofts. And as more-conventional office occupations could increasingly be carried out from homes of any type thanks to the Internet, the idea of home as office also grew. The dot-com boom spawned even more independent, home-based workers looking for spaces like live/work lofts.

The creative live/work loft and work-from-home lifestyle have seemed to merge in digital-age lofts, like those at the Dillon, completed in New York City in 2011. The Dillon offers very polished, open living spaces, with the high ceilings of the old SoHo loft buildings, as well as trophy kitchen appliances. It also offers, like many other recent multiunit projects, such building amenities as business centers and meeting rooms to supplement private space and to support work from home.

1   http://www.ahdli.org/.

2   See Downtown Center Business Improvement District, http://dcbiddata.dev.cartifact.com/
     report/extended?name=&not_sub_cat=enior&statuses%25.

3   "Ralphs Opens First Supermarket in Downtown L.A. in over 50 Years," Progressive Grocer,
     July 20, 2007, http://www.progressivegrocer.com/top-stories/headlines/organic/id22956/
     ralphs-opens-first-supermarket-in-downtown-l-a-in-over-50-years/.

4   "Adaptive Reuse Program Summary," City of Los Angeles.

5   Mike Schulte, "Lofty Ambitions," *Architect's Newspaper*, February 27, 2008.

6   "Smart Growth Illustrated: Downtown Brea, Brea, California," October 14, 2010,
     http://www.epa.gov/smartgrowth/case/brea.htm. See also City of Brea Redevelopment,
     http://www.ci.brea.ca.us/page.cfm?name=econ_dev_redev.

7    $16,842, http://www.vtpi.org/tca/tca0504.pdf; $18,000,
     http://www.mnsu.edu/parking/parking_ramp.html.

8   Pittsburgh's Central Business District saw a population increase of 33.4 percent from
     2000 to 2010 and the number of housing units increased by 44.3 percent
     (PGHSnap http://www.pittsburghpa.gov/dcp/snap/files/PGHSNAP_v2.0_Oct_2011.pdf
     [accessed March 13, 2012]).

Reuse

Rag Flats

Philadelphia, Pennsylvania

Onion Flats
Square feet: 22,685
Completion date: 2006

Above, right: Detail of varied
cladding materials

Opposite: View of the courtyard

Previous: el dorado inc, Finn Lofts,
Wichita, Kansas, 2010, entrance
at dusk

Rag Flats is an experiment in sustainable forms of urban dwelling and a critique of them. The former industrial rag factory has been reconceptualized as a residential garden community, created by using prototypical forms of dwellings commonly found in Philadelphia: the row house, the trinity, the loft, and the pavilion.

Rag Flats intentionally explores the relationships between density, intimacy, and privacy in an urban community. It was a collaborative design/build project undertaken by Minus Studios, Cover, and Onion Flats, with Minus taking on "row" experiments and Cover engaging in custom steel experiments. While each company had its own responsibilities, cross-fertilization between them was frequent throughout the endeavor.

In the process, an inspiring team of architect/builder/craftsmen was forged. This was a significant dimension of Rag Flats, which proposed a mode of thinking and building that was collective, creative, and cohesive rather than specialized, limited, and fragmented.

The Porter House   New York, New York

SHoP Architects
Square feet: 51,460
Completion date: 2003

Right: Original building
and the addition in context

Opposite: Front elevation
from the street

Located in Manhattan's Meatpacking District, the Porter House is the renovation and conversion of a six-story warehouse built in 1905 for residential condominium use. A new 20,000-square-foot addition added four stories to the existing building and an eight-foot cantilever along the building's southern exposure. The development produced twenty residences ranging in size from 900 to 3,400 square feet, as well as a ground-floor commercial space.

A custom-fabricated zinc panel system for the facade and floor-to-ceiling windows of the addition emphasizes the verticality of the structure and creates a unique interface with the original Renaissance Revival exterior. Internally mounted light boxes blur the massing of the building as day turns to night, creating a visual focus from the open urban square at Ninth Avenue and 14th Street. A zinc sidewalk awning wraps the corner and provides signage, shade, and a historical link to the surrounding neighborhood.

497 Greenwich Street   New York, New York

Archi-tectonics / Winka Dubbeldam
Square feet: 77,000
Completion date: 2004

Original warehouse building
and undulating glass facade
of the new addition

Located on the edge of SoHo in New York City, this project involved the renovation of a six-story former warehouse and the addition of a new eleven-story "smart loft" building that wraps up and over it. The new building's main feature is an innovative glass curtain wall, a suspended waterfall of insulated bent glass panels, the first of its kind.

The folded-glass skin of the new structure allows for views of the nearby Hudson River. The building's twenty-three loft apartments offer an open plan and abundant exterior spaces, including balconies and roof terraces on both the west and east facades. The integration of the existing warehouse building with the new steel-and-glass structure mediates between past and present. In the narrow crease between the two structures, cantilevered balconies juxtapose and differentiate between the old and the new, the urban and the private.

Queen of Greene Street

New York, New York

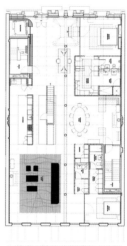

The loft is located in New York's SoHo neighborhood in a nineteenth-century cast-iron building that was restored by its owners, a European couple. The building was renovated to house the showroom for their business on the ground floor, with their own pied-à-terre on the top floor and rooftop, and rental units in between.

The basic structural system of the penthouse interior consists of anodized aluminum building blocks, four feet by four feet by six inches deep, installed inside the shell of the building. These load-bearing panels, which can be used vertically or horizontally, come with an outer skin installed and attached to a stud grid. An additional wood-panel system was developed to create the inner skin of the modules, and another set of perforated panels was produced as a ceiling system.

In its approach the design harks back to the prefabricated cast-iron facades of the SoHo neighborhood but also reflects the owners' interest in technical innovation in design and manufacturing.

**Parallel Design Partnership Limited /
Ali Tayar; Bialosky + Partners**
Square feet: 5,800
Completion date: 2011

Above: Plan

Above, left: Rehabilitated facade

The Piazza at Schmidt's   Philadelphia, Pennsylvania

Erdy McHenry Architecture
Square feet: 165,000
Completion date: 2009

Above, right: Evening view
of the plaza

Opposite, left: Typical
living space

Opposite, right: Street view
of one of the new buildings

The Piazza at Schmidt's, which offers a mix of residential, commercial, and recreational uses, has become an integral part of the regeneration of the Northern Liberties community in Philadelphia. Located on a three-acre portion on the south side of the former Schmidt's Brewery site, this complex includes modern apartment housing, retail and office space, and public amenities. At the center of the project is a large open plaza fronted by shops, galleries, and restaurants.

The 80,000-square-foot plaza is surrounded by three new buildings, which house 260 apartments, five new restaurants, 50,000 square feet of retail space that accommodates thirty-five artisans and boutiques, and 35,000 square feet of office space. At the southern end of the plaza, the facade of an eighty-year-old warehouse that has been rehabilitated into modern apartments serves as a backdrop for live performances.

One York

New York, New York

TEN Arquitectos
Square feet: 136,000
Completion date: 2008

Above: View from Sixth Avenue

Above, right: Typical living space

Opposite: View of the building
in its urban context

Located at the border of Manhattan's Tribeca neighborhood, the One York residential building illustrates the city's constant reinvention of itself. TEN Arquitectos took a squat industrial brick building—which had already been obliquely cut by rerouting along Sixth Avenue—and used it as an adaptable form to be further transmuted.

The nondescript quality and modest scale of the original building were maintained, while its solid massing was cut into and then penetrated by a prismatic glass structure that added six floors' worth of height. Like a quartz vein running through a piece of stone, the addition both fractures the building and holds it together, bringing illumination and clarity to its dense massing. The glass addition is the structure's most profound organizing and aesthetic principle.

The condominiums' floor plans, rather than being fully defined, have been largely determined by the owners themselves, who purchased and carved out portions of the building to suit their needs. The units hover above the city, allowing for a new and unmediated view.

Leavitt Residence

Chicago, Illinois

Miller Hull Partnership
Square feet: 8,600
Completion date: 2008

Opposite, clockwise from left:
detail of the reused brick building
shell; view into the main living
space; vertical sliding glass wall
separating indoors from outdoors

The Leavitt Residence is an extensive transformation of a 1920s mercantile building into a single-family home in the Bucktown neighborhood of Chicago. The original three-story structure consisted of heavy timber framing with brick cladding on the exterior.

The goal of the renovation was to respect the existing building while inserting dramatic new design gestures. The most significant addition was an expansive window wall that extrudes upward and flows over the roof to create a highly transparent penthouse, which serves as the master bedroom. The second major aspect of the building renovation was the replacement of the structurally unstable east facade. The new facade replicates the rhythm of the existing masonry columns, but with a modernist influence at the second level.

Mirroring the triangular footprint of the building, a three-story triangular atrium is at the heart of the home, giving way to massive timber staircases surrounded by cedar and glass. Original beams and exposed brick are juxtaposed with modern cabinetry in the kitchen, once again echoing the tension between old and new.

Finn Lofts

Wichita, Kansas

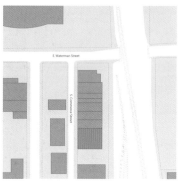

el dorado inc
Square feet: 30,750
Completion date: 2010

Above: Rear facade

Above, right: Street view of the
facade and outdoor area

Finn Lofts is located in the heart of what has come to be known as the Commerce Street Art District in Wichita. The project converts an early twentieth-century warehouse building into a community of dwellings and retail spaces that complements the local art community.

The challenge was to create twenty-seven residential units, all with natural light and ventilation. Originally used as a transfer point for cargo between locomotives and trucks, the existing structure has a large, square floor plate with limited opportunities for apertures to the exterior. The solution was based on the simple notion that light can be incorporated both horizontally and vertically. By understanding the constraints and opportunities of the site and the existing structure, the architects' approach focused on four strategies: adapting, removing, carving, and adding.

346 Congress Street

Boston, Massachusetts

The design of this new infill building reflects the area's ongoing transformation and demonstrates how the district's architecture can be reimagined to meet contemporary needs while respecting the neighborhood's historic integrity.

With its five-story brick facade, the building was inserted into a previously vacant lot next to two fully restored facades of the same height. Together, these create a continuous street wall with a progressive rhythm of windows, architectural details, colors, and materials. Roman brick shapes respond to and complement the Roman bricks of the existing historic buildings, and modern interpretations of historic brick details distinguish the new facade, articulated with a level of detail and depth compatible with the existing buildings and rendered in a new complementary color.

The building's three-story rooftop addition is set back from the street with stepped terraces and inflected walls of glass and metal panel that are "folded" into and over the historic block. This upper addition is expressed in a contemporary architectural language that is influenced by the style and materials of the building's historic context.

Hacin + Associates
Square feet: 140,000
Completion date: 2008

Above, left: Brick facade and modern rooftop addition of the new building

Above, right: Terrace on the rooftop addition

The Bank   Syracuse, New York

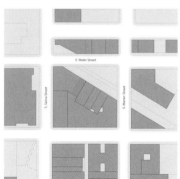

Built in 1898, the Bank of Syracuse was an innovative steel-and-concrete structure designed by Albert Brockway, an associate of architect Ernest Flagg. In successive alterations, the largely vacant building lost most of its ornamental plaster and marble and was divided into a series of low, small offices.

After the building was acquired by its new owner in 2005, it underwent selective demolition that exposed the historic vaulted ceiling of the former banking hall. The program includes a single residence on the upper level, with a kitchen and bath that separate the bedroom from gallery and living space. The first floor is an open loft space that houses an architect's office, and at the ground level is a restaurant.

**Mark Robbins with Fiedler Marciano
Architecture**
Square feet: 6,500
Completion date: 2007

Above, left to right: Street view at night; living space of the residence; living space, view toward kitchen

Opposite: Living space, view toward street

Atrium House　　　Brooklyn, New York

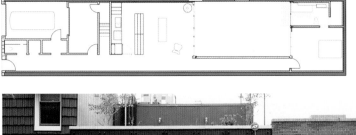

MESH Architectures
Square feet: 2,100
Completion date: 2010

Above, right: Ground-floor plan

Right: Street view

This house, located on a block with a variety of building types, was originally a garage occupying an entire lot. The house is designed to offer a sequence of very different spaces within a small envelope.

The center of the house is two adjacent spaces: a soaring great room and a courtyard with glass on three sides. One enters on an axis that proceeds through the entire length of the house, along a dramatic wall paneled in boards sliced from beams salvaged from the original garage. The space is lit by fixtures made of plumbing pipe and designed by the architects.

The great room, master bedroom, and bathroom open completely onto the courtyard, creating a flowing space when the weather is warm. A garage and recording studio help buffer noise from the busy Brooklyn street. A second bedroom/office and two roof decks occupy the second floor. All the home's systems—including heat, TV, and custom lighting— are controlled from the homeowner's cell phone.

Rieger Hotel Addition

When the owner-residents of the historic Rieger Hotel—a one-hundred-year-old structure that had been restored in 2003—acquired control of an adjacent one-story building and converted it into a garage and workshop, a new structure was necessary to provide elevator and stair access from the garage to the upper residential levels.

When developing the program for the addition, el dorado inc and the client seized the opportunity to add an elegant rooftop garden that affords views of the surrounding skyline. Careful attention was given to detailing the new construction in a simple, subdued manner that complemented the ornate nature of the original building while paying homage to its urban context.

el dorado inc
Square feet: 900
Completion date: 2003

Above, left: Street view of the addition

Above, right: Rooftop garden

Urban
Architecture
Stanley
Saitowitz

Building the City

The central project of architecture is the building of the city. Each contributing part must be more than itself, charging the spaces around it, making connections, adding to the whole. Urban buildings are antidotes to the expressionism of so much current production claiming to be architecture. Rather than self-expression, urban buildings focus on collective form. Rather than plastic configurations of voluntary fantasy, the goal is the continuity of the city. The urban environment is not a series of independent staccato objects floating in a field but a historic process of continuous evolution and development.

The stylistic choice of plastic sculptural form, like Deconstruction or Postmodernism before it, or Art Nouveau or Rococo before them, is on the periphery of the mainstream of architecture and as a movement will become no more than a curiosity despite how many blogs, magazine pages, or crit rooms at schools it currently fills. Such styles are nuances and deviations and contribute little to the building of the city. Rather, they are distractions from this important work at a time when urbanism is growing more rapidly than ever.

Everywhere, new megaprojects are deposited as a kind of punch-drunk architecture of power, destroying any chance for connection and continuity. The idea that cities can be made with anarchic, contrary acts of disconnected formalism is futile. The antithesis of this is the idea of collective form.

These are forms of the built cultural environment that are ancient, regular, and simple, and present a unified view. They have been present since the Stone Age but have continued to evolve into our electronic present.

The most obvious unit of collective form is the cube or rectangular block. It is found as far back as Neolithic times. The block, coupled with the grid as a method of placement, is a universal cultural approach to forming cities.

There are many reasons why making rectangular blocks and placing them in orthogonal grids has become such a useful method. The ability to pack

Previous: Stanley Saitowitz/Natoma Architects, 855 Folsom Street Yerba Buena Lofts, San Francisco, 1998, view from Folsom Street

Opposite: Stanley Saitowitz/Natoma Architects, 1022 Natoma Street, San Francisco, 1992, street view

units together is one reason. It is the simplest ordering of part into whole, implying endless extension without presenting incompleteness. The part and the resulting whole have the same morphology.

Cube and grid have the look of openness, extendability, repeatability, equanimity, directness, publicness. They emerge from clear thought and intention rather than groping expression. They are broad-based cultural infrastructures found throughout time and place.

Cube and grid are the most inert and least organic of forms. They are the most abstract and least anthropomorphic, the most clearly detached from humans, the most distinctly autonomous, the most completely independent of figure, the most easily held in the mind as a form.

Cube and grid remain valuable because they have been in use for so long and continue to offer endless opportunities for transformation.

Building San Francisco

The first things I ever knew about San Francisco were from songs, long before I moved there. Working in a city of songs and being part of building this city has been my focus. I have constantly searched to understand its nature, something I think Ambrose Bierce captured when he wrote, "This city is a point upon a map of fog."

There are 197,000 building parcels in San Francisco, of which 173,000, or 87.8 percent, are residential. Housing is by far the most important element of the city's fabric, so naturally it has been central to our work.

Our first Victorian infill project was our office/loft, built in 1991, followed by a number of other buildings in which we developed prototypes and an approach to urban housing.

Down the street, 1234 Howard uses typical vertical massing, but the texture is achieved with individually operated louvers.

At the Yerba Buena Lofts, the grain of San Francisco streetscapes is expressed in a contemporary way, using the textural and informational quality of Victorians without reference to the actual image.

At 555 Fulton a glass curtain wall is folded in the crenellated bay window pattern to enclose the building.

Stanley Saitowitz/Natoma Architects, 1234 Howard Street, San Francisco, 2007, street view showing the variations created by louvers

The texture of a postcard of San Francisco inspired the vertical fins of the Octavia Gateway, which resembles a billboard image at the entry to the city from the 101 freeway.

At the corner of Larkin and Clay, bar-grating screened porch bays continue the grain of the neighborhood.

Sometimes San Francisco looks like a Mediterranean city, all white and cubic.

Near downtown the fabric changes to taller buildings of brick or terra-cotta or stucco wedding cakes.

Hotels all over the city are wrapped in perforated masonry walls.

I have always been interested in continuity, in buildings that are more than themselves. The subdivision and redivision of land, the grids within grids to the scale of individual units and eventually furniture, is the ordering device of the city. At the Yerba Buena Lofts this urban logic is extruded vertically to become the structure of the building. Each loft is thought of as a stacked lot. The building is a rigorous and repetitive subdivision of plots.

Our urban housing emerges from highly modulated and systematic plans. We use the lessons of mass production, and although there are claims that current technologies will bypass the need for repetition, we have used the economies of serialization to increase quality. We have never had any interest in arbitrary variety, preferring to make all units identical; when inhabited, the neutral spaces we provide result in much more difference than I could ever imagine.

Stanley Saitowitz/Natoma Architects, 855 Folsom Street Yerba Buena Lofts, San Francisco, 1998, loft interior

Indeterminacy

I have always wondered how architecture could be a tool of liberation. Very early in my work, I began to confront the question of indeterminacy versus programming, smooth versus striated space. The first building I built, outside Johannesburg in 1976, was an artist's loft. It was conceived as a scaffold, a frame in which to make a painting. It followed two precedents: the Maison de Verre (in Paris) and the Eames House (in Pacific Palisades, California).

I thought of it as an instrument rather than an object, more like a telephone than a conversation, more like a camera than a photograph.

I was so intent on destroying program that I refused to have a bathroom; a toilet floated behind a corner on one level, a tub sat on another, a shower on another. The dining room was a mobile cart that rolled around the house and out into the garden through the hangar doors.

In our current housing, in order to provide indeterminate deprogrammed space, kitchens and bathrooms are accumulated, collapsed, and minimized. These servant programs are compressed into thickened walls, eliminating the whole idea of rooms and replacing them with minimally differentiated continuous fields. The plans consist of thickened walls and space. The service walls double as structure and align vertically, stacking plumbing. All electrical and sprinkler runs chase within these zones, producing added economies. All lighting emanates from these dense walls. This process of reduction, compression, and repetition provides opportunities for expansion and the reallocation of resources to increase quality in other areas. Through hierarchical unities, elements are assembled, grouped, and minimized, providing the maximum amount of free space for the occupants to determine their own program.

Models

Several models have served as the foundations for our urban housing. In the Case Study Houses of the 1950s, a new modern dwelling emerged in California. Spacious, open, and free, it redefined the domestic landscape as a fluid and continuous field. These houses fully embraced the mechanisms and appliances of modern life, placing them with the same ease as that of furniture. This is the dwelling model we have used for the design of multifamily housing. Density and intensity have their own demands, and the projects we do are the result.

Ever since I first saw that picture in Le Corbusier's *Oeuvre complète* of a hand placing a unit in a large frame, like a bottle in a rack, I have thought of the Unité d'Habitation as the ideal model for the dense contemporary house. Le Corbusier imagined these homes could be premade and stacked, like wine bottles. When I went to Marseilles, I saw that there was something strange about how this piece of city floated in space, like an ocean liner, contextless, but I was amazed by the generosity of the houses within, split on two levels, with two different aspects, and the sense of space despite the dimensions. Later, when Alison and Peter Smithson reworked the Unité at Robin Hood Gardens (now demolished!) in London, giving it an Englishness that related to the texture of the city's row house, I understood the possibility of that method for building a San Francisco Unité. After a few tries, I was able to build the Yerba Buena Lofts, with its modern bay windows.

But the other, more comprehensive influence has been Mies. It is strangely contradictory to look at the work of Mies to understand his significance, because it is most important for what it is not. We value the work for what he managed to purge, remove, exorcise—for the things he rid us of, for the emptiness he made visible.

So we need to look at what is absent, what does not have form, what is not expressed, what is undefined, to grasp the power of his achievement.

Second, we need to consider Mies the urbanist, his contribution to the city, the civilized and compoundable kits of buildings, and the lessons in combining them to form spaces between. This is probably the least acknowledged brilliance of the work—the empty spaces between the buildings. This is probably the most powerful reality of the experience of the buildings—the charged voids formed by the walls of building.

Because of what he did not do, Mies provided the most pervasive model for the metropolis of the twentieth century. Anywhere you go, his example is the one that set the type for the modern city.

The early work is rich with formal exploration, with new geometries derived from science, from art, from engineering. Once in Chicago, the structural frame, the most ubiquitous element of modern architecture, becomes the key formal element. All the explorations and variations are refinements of the architectural language that evolves from this source. All the work reorients to this new context, to the language and technology of the skyscraper, to the curtain wall that wraps the frame, to the evolution and refinement of the elements of metropolitan architecture, to the creation of radical surprise within this established language.

Also absent from the Miesian field is programmatic expression. Office, house, institution: each of these types exposes the structural and spatial realization, not the functional specifics. Each is an essay in general conditions of enclosure, of the constructive relationship of structure and skin, rather than of the interior.

Lake Shore Drive is of course a model, but it is Lafayette Park in Detroit that remains one of the most civilized urban precincts in the United States, setting the bar.

Stanley Saitowitz/Natoma
Architects, Octavia Gateway,
San Francisco, anticipated
completion 2014, building section

Urban Housing Concepts

In our work on housing projects over the years, we have been guided by
the evolution of eight recurring concepts:

1   Urban continuity: constructively building the character of the site—
    not mimicking the surroundings but being proactive in expanding
    and regenerating the context.

2   Indeterminate space: providing the most open and flexible interior
    spaces, with the fewest walls and least programmatic definition, so
    that users have optimal flexibility in personalizing their environment.

3   Compressed services: rationalizing and shrinking the service elements
    to increase free space and make the most efficient, repetitive, and cost-
    effective service cores. We use two strategies for this: thickened walls
    into which all the service elements are swept or pods.

4   Volumetric and horizontal expansion: using continuous and intercon-
    nected areas to amplify the sense of space without increasing square
    footage.

5   Natural light: maximizing the dimensions and strategic location of
    windows to optimize natural daylight.

6   Habitable exterior spaces: providing both private and communal habit-
    able exterior spaces. By carving out exterior spaces, we are able to create
    more opportunities for natural daylighting.

7   Rigorous construction systems: using systematic and repetitive systems to achieve construction economies so that values can be shifted into elements that enhance user experiences.

8   Green: applying both passive and active energy systems, using renewable resources, building lightly using the fewest materials and least effort possible to encompass the most possible volume and space— searching for economy and optimization.

Examples

I was looking for a warehouse we could remodel for our office, but all the buildings I saw needed substantial seismic work. I realized that it was actually going to cost less to build a new building, so I found a lot and persuaded a contractor who was building houses for us to partner with me. This office, at 1022 Natoma Street, was our first building in San Francisco; once it was standing, we had a place to show clients what we could do, and we started receiving other projects for infill housing.

Later we built 1028 Natoma next door, a building where some of the people who work in the office moved into. There I did things I was unable to persuade our developer clients to do. Once they saw it, they realized that there were ways to add value to a building other than by maximizing square footage. Now we are building 1029 Natoma across the street.

A few blocks away is 1234 Howard Street, an eighteen-unit building with a light court running through the block to Natoma Street in the rear. A few blocks from there is 855 Folsom, a 200-unit building that fills much of the block. We have a number of projects at various stages all over the city: 19 Tehama has just been completed; 2020 Ellis is under construction; 8 Octavia Gateway is about to begin; and 1500 South Van Ness, 1875 Mission, 1700 Mission, Sutter, Hubbell, and Jack London Tower are all in various stages of development.

The urban work we have done in San Francisco has led to opportunities to build in other cities, and we are currently completing a pair of large buildings at Case Western Reserve University in Cleveland, which together with the existing fabric makes up a new district. On the ground levels are student services, including a bookstore and grocery store, as well as five restaurants along the alley. Above is rental housing, aimed mostly at a student population. A third building is in design, with a drugstore and student housing for the Cleveland Institute of Art. We are also doing an urban infill project in Toronto, with luxurious units that mostly occupy a full floor.

Stanley Saitowitz/Natoma
Architects, Jack London Tower,
Oakland, California, unbuilt,
rendering showing retail at
street level

Seinfeld Visiting Critic Studio at Syracuse University, Fall 2008

A peninsula is a landmass bordered on three or more sides by water but
still attached to the mainland. The peninsula of San Francisco has developed in a lopsided manner, with all the intense activity on the eastern bay
shore. Downtown, SoMa, and the other wealthy mixed-use neighborhoods
are in this area. The west, on the ocean side, is a monotonous suburban
fabric of residences with occasional main streets and the Richmond and
Sunset districts. In the north is North Beach and the Marina. The south
connects to the mainland and Silicon Valley. There is only one center,
downtown, with varying intensities of neighborhood shopping streets
punctuating the rest of the peninsula. Of the seven square miles that
San Francisco occupies, only two to three are developed as urban fabric.
The rest is low-density detached houses.

Great cities like Tokyo, London, New York, Hong Kong, and Los Angeles
have multiple centers, many nodes, an abundance of intensities.
San Francisco will inevitably grow into such a city, for which this studio
proposes such a multicentered growth.

The progenitor of these new centers is the expansion of BART to serve
other areas of the San Francisco peninsula and vitalize new points on the

map. Six new stops germinate six new districts. Each student will work on one of these six sites. The main question for the studio is to find ways to generate new urban growth by planting the seed of a new center. The Romans had such a formula for building cities: the cardo and decumanus, the grid, the forum, the basilica, the circus, and so forth. These are the questions for the studio: What are the equivalents for our cities today? What kind of building can serve as an urban generator, provoke future development, and act to transform the area into a new urban center? Each of the six sites has an existing unique character to build on, but the focus of the studio is on the provocation of a future: what building type can germinate this evolution, how architecture can be the seed for transformation and urbanization, how a building can be the foundation of the future city.

In this studio we are interested in both continuity and transformation. So much contemporary architecture involves strange landings of alien objects. Instead we will look for ways to develop and connect. We are interested in grand futures founded on the present, in buildings as structure and infrastructure, in new ways to inhabit the crust of the earth that emerge from the present.

Student design from the Seinfeld Studio, 2008, by Manuel Imbert and Ankur S. Patel

Infill

Switch Building   New York, New York

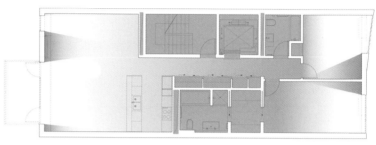

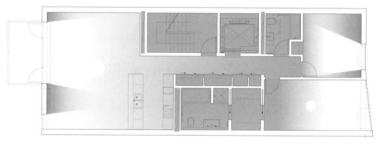

nARCHITECTS
Square feet: 14,500
Completion date: 2007

Above: Balconies on the
rear facade

Above, right: Plans illustrating light
penetration into the building

Opposite: Street view

Previous: LOHA (Lorcan O'Herlihy
Architects), Formosa 1140,
West Hollywood, California, 2009,
rear view

The Switch Building is a seven-story apartment building and art gallery
at 109 Norfolk Street, on the Lower East Side in New York City.
The building consists of four floor-through apartments, a duplex penthouse, and a double-height art gallery on the ground and cellar levels.

The project's design emerged from a creative interpretation of some
of the narrow constraints imposed by zoning and the developer's needs.
In a reinterpretation of a traditional New York bay window, an angled
front facade "switches" back and forth, allowing each floor-through
apartment unique views up and down Norfolk Street while creating
subtle variations in shadows and reflections. From the inside, the bay
windows provide deep window seats surrounded by warm hardwood.

At the rear of each apartment, the living space extends out to
7-by-12 ½-foot balconies—the largest allowed by zoning—which
also shift side to side, creating double-height spaces between balconies
to maximize afternoon light and neighborly interactions. While the
apartment plans are identical, variations in light and views of the city
allow each unit to be distinct.

Hancock Lofts West Hollywood, California

Koning Eizenberg Architecture
Square feet: 133,500
Completion date: 2010

Right: View of the complex from
Hanover Avenue

Opposite, top: Kitchen/dining area
in one of the units

Opposite, bottom: Plan

This four-story, mixed-use complex at Santa Monica Boulevard and
Hancock Avenue includes thirty-one condominium town houses, seven
affordable studios, 11,600 square feet of retail space, sixty-one residential
parking spaces, and 156 city-mandated public parking spaces. The goal
of the design was to achieve a successful balance between the various
aspects of the program, including housing, retail, an active street presence, and parking.

The project's architectural expression is rooted in passive sustainable
strategies. The narrow layouts of the units take full advantage of cross-
ventilation. Apartments facing the boulevard have sliding Mangaris wood
screens that provide exterior shading, minimize heat gain, and allow
inhabitants a choice in their level of engagement with the noisy street
below. The town houses have private courtyards that modulate the scale
as the building moves north to merge with the hillside neighborhood
behind. All units have sealed concrete floors and low-E dual-pane glazing.

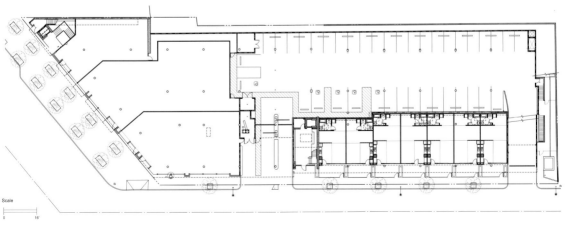

Scale

0   16'

Mezzo

Phoenix, Arizona

Will Bruder + Partners
Square feet: 28,200
Completion date: 2008

Right: Driveway separating
the buildings

Opposite, top: Side view
of the complex

Opposite, bottom: Street view

Mezzo is the result of an enlightened developer client supporting a design approach that grows from the outside in and the inside out. With a total of ten units, the condominium complex fits distinctively into its 1950s midtown Phoenix residential neighborhood. Five units are entered from the east through street-side garden courtyards defined by weathered, welded wire mesh. The other five are accessed from the west along a common "mews" walkway. At the heart of the complex are a shared auto court and a raised-bed community vegetable garden.

Each home of 1,525 square feet provides for an entry area, a homework/play area, and a carport at level one; living, dining, and kitchen areas at level two; and two bedroom-and-bath suites at level three. Constructed of expressed masonry bearing walls and wood frame, the units' simply sculpted spaces are given identity by the use of carefully positioned window apertures, which are shaded by perforated metal scrims, and triangular pop-out kitchen bay windows. The angular geometry of the interior walls adds to the dynamism of the interiors.

2281 Glisan

Portland, Oregon

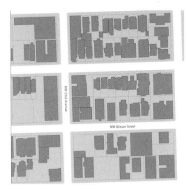

Allied Works Architecture
Square feet: 14,000
Completion date: 2000

Above: Main living space of
the residence

Above, right: Upstairs landing

Opposite: Street view at dusk

This mixed-use building is located in a historic retail and residential neighborhood in Portland, Oregon. Set behind a veil of street trees, the building incorporates office and retail spaces on the lower three floors, with a multi-level private residence and roof garden overlooking the city. A skin of glass, slate, stainless-steel mesh panels, and stone tile wraps the structural frame and extends to the limits of the zoning volume. Floor-to-ceiling glass on two exposures maximizes light within while revealing the structure beyond. The mesh panels modulate the glass on the south and east sides, acting as a visual screen to terraces and as rails for operable windows.

The ground-floor retail space opens to the street through an uninterrupted wall of glass. Above, a metal-clad canopy extends the width of the building, defining the exterior public domain and offering protection from the elements. In the penthouse, a modern palette of wood, steel, and stone creates a neutral field for the resident's collection of art and furnishings.

Glenmore Gardens   Brooklyn, New York

As part of the New Foundations program for the Department of Housing Preservation and Development (HPD), Della Valle Bernheimer, acting as both developer and architect, coordinated the design and construction of ten semidetached, two-family homes in the East New York section of Brooklyn. Designed to encourage developers to build affordable housing, the 2,200-square-foot homes were privately constructed on land owned by the HPD as part of Mayor Michael Bloomberg's $7.5 billion plan to create 165,000 units of affordable housing over a ten-year period.

The two-and-a-half-story units consist of two owner-occupied apartments and two rental apartments. A simple 90-degree turn in the direction of the corrugated aluminum along the party walls created an identifiable difference between the homes. Painted fiber-cement panels and cedar siding were used to articulate punched openings that surround the windows and entry doors. An embedded cedar box at the second floor of the building represents the differentiation between the owner's unit and the rental property, which sits at street level. On the third floor, a small outdoor terrace abuts the master bedroom, giving the owners a panoramic view of their newly rebuilt neighborhood.

Della Valle Bernheimer
Square feet: 20,500
Completion date: 2006

Above: Cladding detail

Opposite: Street view

The George

Phoenix, Arizona

Studio Ma
Square feet: 19,200
Completion date: 2010

Above: One of the eight
single-family units

Above, right: Dining area
in one of the units

Opposite, top: Rear view
of the garages

Opposite, bottom: Plan

Named after George Christiansen, the architect whose house once occupied the site, the George consists of eight single-family attached units arranged in four groups of two units each.

The project provides family-oriented amenities, including 2,200 square feet of living area, three bedrooms, two and a half baths, a family room, a ground-floor living/dining area, and a two-car garage. Second-floor decks enhance the indoor/outdoor quality of the design while providing visual interest in the outdoor public spaces.

The project utilizes affordable design strategies for achieving sustainability, including the use of rainwater captured and diverted to irrigate low-water planting areas, controlled daylighting, and exterior cladding made with recycled content.

Perforated metal and planted green screens provide varying degrees of privacy throughout the community, while juxtaposed materials fold in and out of corners, camouflaging the units and breaking down the scale of the project. A dynamic composition of weathered and bright metal skins picks up on the colors and textures of the neighborhood's pecan tree–lined streets and the dark rust color of the Arizona mesquite.

Gardner 1050   West Hollywood, California

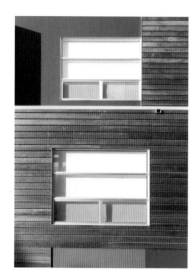

LOHA (Lorcan O'Herlihy Architects)
Square feet: 27,000
Completion date: 2006

Above: Wood cladding detail

Above, right: Street view of
the complex

Located in the eastern section of West Hollywood, Gardner 1050 is a result of studies in reinvigorating existing housing typologies to create new opportunities for living within the extremely tight economic and spatial parameters of the speculative housing market. This project explores alternative approaches to the courtyard housing typology.

Weaving the buildings' circulation into a spectrum of public space, the central courtyard allows all residents to have direct access to their units from the exterior and eliminates the need for mechanically climate-controlled corridors. In an effort to extend the courtyard vertically, stainless-steel cables creep up to the third-level walkways, forming scaffolding for a "hanging" garden. This foliage, which includes native drought-tolerant species, extends the landscape to the floors above while filtering the strong California sunlight.

Formosa 1140   West Hollywood, California

Located in the heart of West Hollywood, this new eleven-unit housing project emphasizes the central importance of shared open space for the residents and the community. Formosa takes what would be the internalized open space of the courtyard and moves it to the exterior of the building to create a park that occupies approximately one-third of the project site.

By pushing the building to one side and creating a linear organization of the living units, the architects provided each apartment with park frontage and ample cross ventilation. External corridors, articulated through layers of perforated metal and small openings, serve as a buffer between public and private realms. The careful placement of outer panels and inner fenestration creates a choreographed effect, both revealing and concealing; the exterior skin also keeps west-facing units cooler by acting as a screen and shading device.

The provision of the public park space led to a series of negotiations between the developers, the architects, and the City of West Hollywood that resulted in the leasing of the park to the City as part of a network of pocket parks.

LOHA (Lorcan O'Herlihy Architects)
Square feet: 16,000
Completion date: 2009

Above, left: Street view

Above, right: Main living area of one of the units

The Schermerhorn

Brooklyn, New York

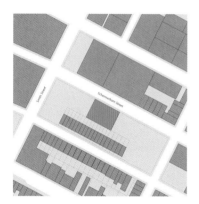

Ennead Architects
Square feet: 98,000
Completion date: 2009

Right: Conference space

Opposite, clockwise from top:
Residential floor plan; typical living
area; rehearsal space; street view

The Schermerhorn seeks to define a new paradigm for subsidized housing in New York City. Developed by Common Ground Community in cooperation with the Actors Fund, the building provides supportive housing for single adults transitioning out of homelessness, people living with HIV/AIDS, and low-income community residents, with preference given to those employed in the performing-arts and entertainment industry. The building is part of an overall block development on the edge of downtown Brooklyn, in Boerum Hill.

Individualized support services are provided to help tenants maintain their housing, address health issues, and pursue education and employment. Each of the nine residential floors offers twenty studio units and a suite containing four single-room-occupancy units with two shared bathrooms and a common kitchen.

Principles of sustainability have informed the design and selection of systems and materials for the project. The building's primary facade features a channel glass wall fabricated with a high percentage of postconsumer-waste glass. Low-E glazing is used in all other windows and curtain wall systems, and the green roof terrace on the second floor minimizes the heat island effect.

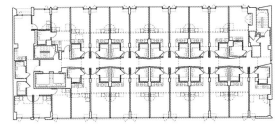

The Dillon   New York, New York

Smith-Miller + Hawkinson Architects
Square feet: 176,000
Completion date: 2011

Right: Street view

Far right: Rooftop view of
the building in its urban context

The Dillon provides a varied fabric for city living, paying homage both to the ubiquitous New York City brownstone block and to Le Corbusier's Ville Radieuse, as well as such descendants as Gordon Bunshaft's Manhattan House, James Freed's Kips Bay Towers, and Oskar Stonorov's housing for New York University.

As an extensive low-rise and midblock project, the building replaces open parking lots and derelict structures with an optimistic premise drawn in part from Jane Jacobs's observations of city life. In an innovative response to the restrictive zoning, this through-block site hosts both the customary residential tower with repeating floor plans and an atypical model: a bar building combining maisonettes, skip-stop duplexes, and triplexes with rooftop cabanas, all served by underground self-parking facilities. The assemblage of these elements results in an extremely economical building section and presents a new typology for urban living.

PRD 845

Phoenix, Arizona

PRD 845 is an urban infill project in downtown Phoenix, close to the Roosevelt historic and arts districts. The site was originally an empty lot, measuring three-quarters of an acre, adjacent to a commercial development near one of the two primary intersections giving access to the downtown area.

A sensitive cluster of twelve condominium homes, this enclave is organized around two private "mews" that mix cars and people in an intimate urban-type environment. Units range in size from 900 to 2,200 square feet and are designed to accommodate an active, live/work lifestyle, with ground-floor garage/studio spaces and large outdoor rooftop decks with views of downtown Phoenix and the surrounding mountains. The folded roof plane creates volumetric slots throughout the complex, giving it a distinctive skyline profile.

Carefully chosen building materials complement the Southwest desert environment. An innovative rain-screen wall, made of low-mass, corrugated, fiber-reinforced concrete panels on furring channels, allows accumulated heat to escape through a slot at the top of the wall.

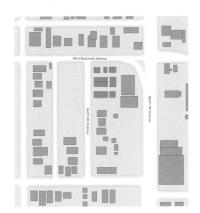

Studio Ma
Square feet: 24,000
Completion date: 2008

Above, left: Street view

Above, right: Typical dining area

Court-Houses   Miami, Florida

K/R Architect and John Bennett, Architect
Square feet: 6,400
Completion date: 2006

Above: Movies projected onto a wall in the courtyard

Above, right: Central court between the two residences

While there are many precedents for the "court-house" structure, in Mies's studio it evolved as a series of glass-enclosed, single-story spaces that look out onto open-air courts and green areas, all contained compactly within a surrounding rectangular wall.

This project, the Miami Court-Houses, was intended as a field test of Mies's theoretical investigations, which he never fully concluded in his built work. The plans of the two houses are mirrored along a party wall and frame a fifty-foot live oak that dominates the previously vacant lot in a neighborhood of cottages built in the 1920s and '30s.

Two glass-enclosed pavilions—one with living, dining, and kitchen spaces, the other with bedrooms—face each other across a central court. The court is divided by a lap pool spanned by a concrete bridge. Two additional open courts, heavily planted, provide alternative perspectives toward the front and rear of the houses. The inward orientation of the houses and their fluid interiors offer a sense of spaciousness and privacy unexpected on such a small parcel of land.

26th Street Affordable Housing

Santa Monica, California

Kanner Architects
Square feet: 42,000
Completion date: 2007

Far left: Stairwells and hallways
on the interior face of the
building

Left: Street view

This low- to moderate-income family-housing project at 26th Street
and Santa Monica Boulevard is the product of an exhaustive community outreach mission. The final design includes input from the City of
Santa Monica and the community at large, and takes into consideration
the region's mild climate as well as historical precedents of Southern
California modernist architecture.

The building comprises forty-four units and a community room.
The bright landscaped courtyard was designed to encourage family and
community interaction. Living spaces are organized in a linear fashion
to facilitate cross ventilation from nearby ocean breezes, eliminating the
need for energy-intensive rooftop air-conditioning equipment.

The design incorporates dual-glazed and laminated windows along both
street-facing sides to eliminate exterior noise. Dry wells collect and disperse
stormwater runoff and minimize the project's impact on the city's sewer
system. The eighty-one subterranean parking spaces—accessed from an
alley to minimize traffic issues—exceed the minimum number required.

Casa Feliz

San Jose, California

Rob Quigley
Square feet: 25,300
Completion date: 2009

Above: Street view

Above, right: Aerial view of the
building in its context

Casa Feliz replaced an aging residential hotel near downtown San Jose
with sixty new efficiency apartments. The project serves extremely
low-income tenants and residents with developmental disabilities.

The tight infill site, less than a half acre, required a creative and efficient
design. Four stories of housing are located over a single level of below-grade
parking for twenty-two cars. Amenities include a group activity room,
a lounge, a common kitchen, computer stations, an on-site laundry, and
communal porches and decks. The two-story lobby, flooded with natural
light, lends dignity and grandeur to this domestically scaled project.
These areas connect visually with the outdoor spaces and circulation core
on the upper floors, enhancing social interaction among residents.

The owner's commitment to creating a sustainable building—which features
San Jose's first living roof—was recognized with a LEED Gold rating.

Art Stable

Seattle, Washington

Art Stable is an urban infill project in the rapidly developing South Lake Union neighborhood of Seattle. Built on the site of a former horse stable, the seven-story, mixed-use building carries its working history into the future with highly adaptable live/work units. Both the front and back elevations of the building are active. The alley-facing facade features a hinge that is eighty feet tall, topped by a davit crane and five steel-clad, hand-cranked doors that make up nearly a third of the facade. This system of moving oversize objects into the building refers to that of traditional warehouses.

Units are designed to accommodate flexibility of use and changes over time, and are zoned for both residential and commercial use. The shell and core of the building are built to last for more than one hundred years. The concrete structure is designed to take heavy loads, and structural and mechanical systems are exposed. Geothermal loops were inserted into the building's structural piles, resulting in an innovative and highly energy-efficient radiant heating and cooling system. This is one of the first examples of the use of this type of geothermal system in this country.

The building's simple, no- and low-maintenance materials—including concrete, steel, and glass—draw on the warehouse typology of the formerly industrial neighborhood. The interior layouts are determined by each unit's owners, who can punch windows into the north facade of the building, creating a personalized balance between privacy and transparency. The building draws on the architectural concepts of prospect and refuge, transposed to an urban setting.

Olson Kundig Architects
Square feet: 32,000
Completion date: 2010

Above: Front entrances

The Brook

Bronx, New York

Alexander Gorlin Architects
Square feet: 90,000
Completion date: 2010

Above: Green roof

Above, right: Main facades

This new facility spans an infill block that defines the corner of 148th Street and Brook Avenue, creating a street wall where an empty lot formerly existed. The building holds 198 permanent supportive housing units for the previously homeless and people with HIV/AIDS, and acts as a temporary residence for young people transitioning to permanent employment and homes. Offices for caseworkers and social service agencies, as well as a computer lab, an exercise room, a medical office, meeting rooms, a laundry, and a community room, are also incorporated. The L-shaped plan includes a courtyard in the rear, which mitigates street noise and creates a sense of intimacy and serenity within the urban setting. Open terraces and a green roof provide places to gather, encouraging the development of community.

The building is designed and engineered for maximum environmental sensitivity, using the most cost-effective means available. Green features include heating and cooling systems controlled by motion sensors, a green roof irrigated by recycled gray water, low-flow showerheads, and Energy Star appliances. Low- and non-VOC flooring, paints, and primers are used throughout the interior.

Alligator

New Orleans, Louisiana

This affordable home arose from post-Katrina rehousing efforts in Central City, New Orleans, an impoverished neighborhood situated between the central business district and the prosperous uptown area.

An unusually narrow lot width of nineteen feet resulted in a 13-foot-wide, 960-square-foot scheme with two bedrooms and one and a half bathrooms. Nicknamed "Alligator" because of its "open-mouth" profile, the house is based on the traditional shotgun layout, with all the rooms aligned in a row, front to back. In this design, however, a set of rolling doors allows for privacy and passage to the rear bedroom and bath.

The house includes a stoop with metal grate steps that offer a casual spot to sit and visit. The street facade is clad in translucent white plastic panels containing fluorescent fixtures. The home has insulated windows that not only meet hurricane resistance requirements but also form an energy- and cost-efficient thermal envelope. The exterior walls and roof are clad in factory-painted, preformed metal siding for easy maintenance and long-term durability.

Funds for the project were provided largely by a client of buildingstudio, who wanted to support rebuilding efforts in post-Katrina New Orleans.

buildingstudio
Square feet: 960
Completion date: 2009

Above, left: Street view

Above, right: Plan

Thin Flats

Philadelphia, Pennsylvania

Onion Flats/Plumbob
Square feet: 16,000
Completion date: 2009

Above: Roof gardens

Above, right: Street view

Opposite, clockwise from left: rear view;
staircase of a typical unit; street view

This eight-unit residential building explores the latent architectural potential hidden in the traditional form of the Philadelphia row house. The vertical
rhythm, regularity, and simultaneous diversity of this ubiquitous urban residential typology served as the primary sources of inspiration for Thin Flats.

Thin faces fronting the streets mask and blur conventional lines of demar-
cation between the duplex dwellings. In the process, a degree of density
emerges along with an expansiveness that is uncommon in the thin space
of the typical Philadelphia row, which is often light deficient and insular at
its core. Thin Flats questions these inadequacies by reconfiguring the
relationship between the interior and the skin to flood the core with light
and air. This skin also affords each room on the periphery an outdoor
space while remaining within the envelope.

The facade of the lower units is pushed back from the sidewalk to accommodate circulation, provide basement spaces with light, aid in solar shading,
and create a veil from public view. Balconies on upper floors are recessed
behind the surface of the veil to encourage interaction among neighbors.

1028 Natoma Street   San Francisco, California

Stanley Saitowitz/Natoma Architects
Square feet: 6,900
Completion date: 2006

Above: Kitchen area of one
of the units

Above right and opposite:
Street views

This infill project was built on a 25-by-80-foot lot in San Francisco's South of Market neighborhood. Parking and an entrance lobby are at street level; above are four stacked residential units. One thickened party wall provides vertical access and a light court. The other acts as a service zone, condensing kitchens, bathrooms, laundry, and storage behind sliding glass doors. Floating walls divide the free space in the center, which is finished with a variety of materials, all in different shades of white.

The front facade has a bay-window silhouette constructed of horizontal aluminum bar grating, which provides both shading for the southern exposure and a veil shielding the city beyond. The surfaces behind the bay are sheathed in perforated metal.

Notes on
Contributors

Andrew Bernheimer is the principal of Brooklyn-based Bernheimer Architecture. He was a founding partner of the firm Della Valle Bernheimer and is assistant professor and director of the MArch program at Parsons The New School for Design. Bernheimer's work has been the subject of many articles and publications, including the monograph *Think/ Make* (2009). His work has received awards from the General Services Administration, AIA New York, and AIA Los Angeles.

Vishaan Chakrabarti is Marc Holliday Associate Professor of Real Estate Development and director of the Center for Urban Real Estate at Columbia University's Graduate School of Architecture, Planning & Preservation, as well as a partner at SHoP Architects. He was previously an executive vice president at the Related Companies, director of the Manhattan Office for the New York Department of City Planning, and director of Urban Design at Skidmore, Owings & Merrill.

Julie Eizenberg is a founding principal of Koning Eizenberg Architecture in Santa Monica, California. The firm's work has been extensively published and exhibited and has earned more than ninety design awards. In 2009 Koning Eizenberg was selected as the AIA California Council Firm of the Year, and in 2012 Eizenberg was awarded the AIA Los Angeles Gold Medal. Eizenberg teaches and lectures around the world and is the author of *Architecture Isn't Just for Special Occasions* (2006).

Douglas Gauthier is a principal at GAuthier Architects. His projects include multiscale residential and institutional projects in New York City as well as BURST*008, a full-scale house commissioned by the Museum of Modern Art for its exhibition Home Delivery. Gauthier has been featured in *Architectural Record*, *Architecture*, and *Time*, and has published articles in *Architectural Design*, *Another Pamphlet*, and *Material Evidence*.

Jonathan Massey is trained as an architect and historian and is Meredith Professor for Teaching Excellence at Syracuse University, where he has chaired the BA program and the University Senate. A cofounder of the

Transdisciplinary Media Studio and the Aggregate Architectural History Collaborative, he has published in many journals and essay collections and is the author of *Crystal and Arabesque* (2009).

Philip Nobel is an architect as well as an architecture and design critic. He has written for *Architectural Digest, Artforum, Metropolis,* the *Nation,* the *New York Times, Vogue,* and other publications, and is the author of *Sixteen Acres* (2005). He practices with the firm Nobel & de Monchaux.

Gregg Pasquarelli is a founding partner of SHoP Architects in New York. He studied architecture at Columbia University and has since taught at Yale University, Columbia, the University of Virginia, and the University of Florida. He lectures globally and his work has been reviewed and published in periodicals such as *Architect, Architectural Record, Dwell, Metropolis,* and the *New York Times,* among others.

Mark Robbins is executive director of the International Center of Photography and the former dean of the Syracuse University School of Architecture. He served as director of design at the National Endowment for the Arts, was curator of architecture at the Wexner Center for the Arts, and was an associate professor in the Knowlton School of Architecture at The Ohio State University. He is the author of *Households* (2006).

Stanley Saitowitz is professor emeritus of architecture at the University of California, Berkeley, and principal of Stanley Saitowitz/Natoma Architects in San Francisco. He was the 1998 recipient of the AIA Henry Bacon Medal for Memorial Architecture. Saitowitz's work has been published internationally and is featured in the books *Stanley Saitowitz* (Architecture at Rice 33, 1995), *Stanley Saitowitz: A House in the Transvaal* (1996), and *Stanley Saitowitz: Buildings and Projects* (2005).

Peggy Tully is a landscape architect and urban designer. She is currently a research fellow at Syracuse University's School of Architecture, where she studies the postindustrial city and the relationship between poverty and the built environment. Tully is also editor of *From the Ground Up: Innovative Green Homes* (2012) in the New City Books series.

Illustration Credits

14–15, 30: Daniel Kariko

25: Getty Images

29: Courtesy of Scott Evans

33: Laura Migliorino

49–53: Bernheimer Architecture

56: Richard Barnes

59, 72: Studio Gang

60–61 Herzog & de Meuron

62–63: Brininstool + Lynch

64–65: Office dA

66–67: Dirk Denison Architects

68–69: Lindy Roy/Roy Co.

70–71: Neil M. Denari Architects, Inc.

73 left, 128–29: Frank Oudeman

73 right: Evan Joseph

75, 77: Iwan Baan

76: Stanley Saitowitz/Natoma Architects

79, 83–91: Koning Eizenberg Architecture

80: Christine McMahan and Eric Zahn

95, 108: Mike Sinclair

96–97: Onion Flats

98–99: Seong Kwon

100: Floto & Warner Photography

101: Joshua McHugh

102: Peter Kubilus

103 left: Timothy Hursley

103 right: Roman Torres

104–5: TEN Arquitectos

107: Marty Peters Photography

109: Bruce T. Martin

110: Courtesy of Mark Robbins

111: Stewart Cairns

112: MESH Architectures

113: el dorado inc

115–24: Stanley Saitowitz/Natoma Architects

125: Manual Imbert and Ankur S. Patel

127, 140–41: Lawrence Anderson/Esto

130–31: Eric Staudenmaier

132–33, 138–39: Bill Timmerman

134–35: Hélène Binet

136–37: Della Valle Bernheimer

142: Albert Vecerka/Esto

143: David Sundberg/Esto

144: Michael Moran

145: Michael Weschler Photography

146: Annie Schlechter

147: Kanner Architects

148: Rob Quigley

149: Benjamin Benschneider

150: Alexander Gorlin Architects

151: Undine Prohl

152–53: Mariko Reed

154–55: Tim Griffith